"What a beautiful and challenging book! I was able to witness some of the aftermath of the storm firsthand. Your book brought to life not only the utter devastation but also the sparkle of hope that remains in those who have found something deeper as a result of their tragedy. Thank you for giving such a clear picture of your pain, and the loss of so many, while also bringing to mind the redemptive shards that can still be found in the midst of those who lived through the horror. Your ability to acknowledge the 'storms within' and yet to overcome is remarkable."
　—Mae Elise Cannon, director of Development and Transformation
　　　　Extension Ministries, Willow Creek Community Church

"In *Soul Storm*, Bruce Smith grasps the essence of the spiritual struggle that is reflected in the recent hurricane tragedy in our state. For those who have faced or are facing troubled times, this book will strike a chord of hope and strength in the place of despair."
　—Dino Rizzo, lead pastor, Healing Place Church,
　　　　Baton Rouge, Louisiana

"Our world is all too acquainted with disasters of all kinds. Katrina and her impact is one catastrophe that will remain in our national consciousness for years to come. The sheer scope, geographically, economically, and spiritually, is beyond any natural disaster we have experienced as Americans. *Soul Storm* offers us insight, hope, and meaning in the aftermath of this historic storm. As Bruce reminds us, even in the worst of circumstances God is on the move. We are reminded in this work that God is still in control and He can be found where we least expect to find Him."
　—Mike Ennis, director of Strategic Initiatives,
　　Convoy of Hope, a nonprofit worldwide relief organization

"What a timely reminder that when the rains come and all seems lost, our hope is found in the God of our salvation. I commend Bruce for an honest, thoughtful, and reflective account of the tragedy we've all been touched by. We too are rebuilding after Katrina and anticipating the beauty that will be fashioned out of this tragedy."
　—Danny Wuerffel, executive director of Desire Street Ministries,
　　　　former Heisman Trophy winner and NFL quarterback

"A very personal reflection on life's storms, the survivor instinct, and the innate need in each of us to sort out the moral reason why. Very refreshing."

> —Gene Mills, Louisiana Family Forum,
> president of PRC Compassion

"Your parallels to scripture are frightening and inspirational. Everyone who is a part of coming back from an event like Katrina could find healing in reading this book. It was a breath of fresh air."

> —Lucy Bustamante, WWL-TV news anchor, New Orleans

"Bruce Smith takes us into both the literal Katrina and its devastating effect and into all the 'Katrinas' that buffet our lives. Most especially, *Soul Storm* takes us beyond the Katrinas of life to show us the hope and new life of the resurrection, not only of the body, but of the soul."

> —Robert Webber, Northern Seminary

"Bruce Smith gives an eyewitness report of the death and destruction caused by Hurricane Katrina. But Bruce doesn't stop with the telling of property devastation, disrupted lives, and total loss of personal belongings. He chronicles how God challenged some displaced residents to look beyond the devastation and loss to recovery and building a better future. Bruce Smith's deep faith enabled him to see beyond the natural realm and translate biblical principles into practical realities to help victims become victors . . . an inspiring message of hope to all who suffer devastation and loss."

> —Rev. George Ekeroth, director, Assemblies of God
> International Fellowship

"No one likes pain. But pain communicates to us the need to change. This book reflects a serious work of heart from author Bruce Smith. He demonstrates wisdom beyond his years, which makes me think that this work carries a coauthor of the Holy Spirit. I believe anyone dealing with the problem of pain will find this an excellent resource for instruction and personal growth."

> —Justin N. Fennell, comedian, consultant, speaker

"Wise followers of Jesus Christ will hear the message of Katrina, delivered so splendidly in *Soul Storm*, and cling to the cross as their anchor in the torrents. For all of us, the gray clouds will build and the rains will come at some point in our lives. It's a guarantee. Do you need to read this book? Only if you're breathing."

—Todd Masson, editor, *Louisiana Sportsman Magazine*

"The quest for equity and parity in the nation is an ongoing process, and not even Katrina, as catastrophic as it was, will ignite an overnight shift in the hearts of men. However, your book creates the ongoing dialogue for a conversation regarding true change and partnership between the races, cultures, and religions. I applaud your doing God's will."

—Dr. Rodney S. Sampson,
MBA, founder of *World Christian Times*

"I really admire and appreciate your sense of unsinkable optimism."

—Mark Mittelberg, best-selling author and speaker

"In this book we find that broken dreams, destruction, fear, and misery can actually catapult people of faith toward God's best. Bruce reminds us, as a people and as a country, that only in turning toward God can we find a passion and purpose for rebuilding our lives amidst disaster."

—Dr. William Hamel, president, Evangelical Free Church of America

"The most obvious virtue of Bruce Smith's book is [its] scope. There is something here for everyone—on-the-scene narratives from the Katrina disaster, autobiography, excursions into literature, philosophic reflection, biblical analysis, and meditations on the meaning of suffering."

—Dr. Leland Ryken, C. S. Lewis Scholar, Wheaton College

"This is the message our people, our city, and our nation need right now. Bruce has offered us words of healing written with artistry. Like a great jazz composition, this deserves a hearing. The section on Coltrane is right on."

—Jason Marsalis and Ellis Marsalis

SOUL STORM

SOUL STORM

FINDING GOD AMIDST DISASTER

REFLECTIONS FROM A HURRICANE KATRINA SURVIVOR

BRUCE LEE SMITH

PELICAN PUBLISHING COMPANY

GRETNA 2006

*The word "Pelican" and the depiction of a pelican are trademarks
of Pelican Publishing Company, Inc., and are registered in the
U.S. Patent and Trademark Office.*

Library of Congress Cataloging-in-Publication Data

Smith, Bruce Lee.
  Soul storm : finding God amidst disaster / Bruce Lee Smith.
    p. cm.
  ISBN-13: 978-1-58980-440-1 (hardcover : alk. paper)
  ISBN-13: 978-1-58980-442-5 (hardcover with cd : alk. paper) 1.
Consolation. 2. Suffering--Religious aspects--Christianity. 3.
Providence and government of God. I. Title.
  BV4905.3.S62 2006
  248.8'6--dc22
                                        2006015103

Unless otherwise indicated, all Scripture quotations are taken from *The Holy Bible,
English Standard Version.* Copyright © 2000; 2001 by Crossway Bibles, a division
of Good News Publishers. Used by permission. All rights reserved.

Scripture quotations marked NIV are taken from the *Holy Bible, New International
Version®, NIV®.* Copyright © 1973, 1978, 1984 by International Bible Society.
Used by permission of Zondervan. All rights reserved.

Scripture quotations marked NKJV are taken from the *New King James Version.*
Copyright © 1982 by Thomas Nelson, Inc. Used by permission. All rights
reserved.

Scripture quotations marked KJV are taken from the *King James Version* of the Bible.

Printed in the United States of America

Published by Pelican Publishing Company, Inc.
1000 Burmaster Street, Gretna, Louisiana 70053

Contents

Concluding Remarks: God and Disaster

Introduction

"Disaster." The word itself is unsettling. "Catastrophe." The word immediately brings stress, anxiety, depression. "Storm." The imagery carries fear, danger, and havoc on its winds. Such is the reality of all of our lives. How do we make sense of a world seemingly filled with pain, loss, and destruction? Can any *good* news be found? More critically, can there be a *good* force behind any of this? What do we do and where do we turn when the world around us brings turmoil into our lives and souls? Amidst the storms that rage around us and within us can there be any meaning, peace, and hope? When divorce, death, loss, struggle, and illness (mental or physical) threaten to overwhelm us, can we find rescue, a rescuer?

The world has spent some time now witnessing the impact of Hurricane Katrina. On the heels of her wrath, CNN and other news agencies have brought us multiple stories of regular disasters. The fires in Texas, the cyclone in Australia, the earthquake in Pakistan, tornadoes in the heart of our country, and so many other disasters continue to engage the national and worldwide audience on this planet's predicament and its purpose. The news media has captured the "before and after" of these incidents. The ramifications of these "natural" disasters are clearly enormous, and in all likelihood, more than we yet know. Geographically, economically, psychologically, and spiritually, the scope of these events is enormous. The hundreds of billions of dollars needed to address this level of destruction are mind-boggling. We are forced to ask why these things happen, what they mean, and how those caught in the grips of these realities are to move forward.

One city, recently in the news, has directed the focus of people's hearts and minds around the globe on the reality of disaster: New Orleans. This is my city, and her struggle for survival and meaning has much to say to us as individuals, as a society, and as a nation. As she fights for her life she will teach all of us many things about ourselves. This book, it should be stated early on, is about much more than one city, one disaster, or one event. It is about the soul — the soul of a person, of a people, of a planet. Yet, because we must start somewhere, and because the enormity of this disaster has captured us all in recent days, we begin here with my town, New Orleans. She is a good picture of each of us in so many ways. Her beauty, charm, character, and spirit resemble our individual and national soul just as her vile habits, immoral pursuits, and thirst for pleasure resemble the darkness found in the recesses of our national and individual hearts. We are introduced to the topic at hand by her, but we shall travel much further across the landscape of our souls as we take this journey through the storms of life. My hope for you, as you read, is that in this journey you will find your life's compass and the Lover of your soul.

New Orleans is a city with a soul. On August 29, 2005, the soul of this jewel of a city experienced the force of a storm never before seen in this country. A great American city now lies in ruins. Much has been lost, and thousands upon thousands have felt the depth of despair. The stench, the gray dust that still covers parts of the city, and the eerie silence in once thriving neighborhoods remain as reminders of Katrina's cruel wrath. This historic storm and her devastating impact upon the Gulf Coast area have affected all of us emotionally, spiritually, and economically. How do we make sense of this calamity? How do we resolve the questions in our minds regarding life's ultimate purpose when it is so hard to image a catastrophe like this having any purpose at all? What was Katrina's message? What are we to learn from this storm? Where do we go from here? These and other critical questions that arise from the rubble of Hurricane Katrina, from the waters of our world's floods, tsunamis, fires, and earthquakes are the focus of this book. This is a story of disaster and yet one of hope. This is a story of soul survival. Our quest in the pages of this book is to find God amidst disaster. Along the way, we will come to see that He is the One who actually finds us.

I am a New Orleans native. I lived through Katrina. I am still living through Katrina. Now called the largest natural disaster in American history, this hurricane decimated an enormous geographical area on the Gulf Coast. Though I live thirty miles north of the city of New Orleans, and though I got out early, the impact upon my life and those close to me has been huge. Members of my own family found themselves on rooftops awaiting rescue. Watching the devastation and carnage in our cities from places far from our home during the months after the storm was profoundly difficult. There is so much to process, so many things to work through, so many ideas, thoughts, feelings, and uncertainties. The shock, numbness, pain, loss, and fear swirl around from moment to moment much like Katrina's winds. As intense as the storm itself, the storm within us continues to rage long after the bad weather has subsided. Months after the storm has "passed," many families are trying to figure out how to "do" life from this moment forward. This is true for anyone who has experienced the storms of the soul. Whether a child has been lost to leukemia or a spouse's love has been stolen away, the ensuing chaos buffets the heart, mind, body, and soul in ways we could never have comprehended prior to the storm's landfall.

As we have witnessed recent tragedies unfolding, and others before (9-11, Columbine, Oklahoma City, etc.), we have witnessed scenes that defy our understanding. Recently, the images we all witnessed in New Orleans and the stories that have been told are profoundly disturbing. Dead bodies floating in putrid waters have been broadcast worldwide via CNN. New Orleans police officers abandoned their posts and some even committed suicide as they were overcome with grief. Children have been separated from families, lives have been lost, homes have been destroyed, and jobs have vanished for so many caught in the crosshairs of this historic storm. Entire communities are gone, neighborhoods are unrecognizable, churches have drowned in the floodwaters, and the scattering of families and friends across America has changed our relational networks forever. What is happening? Why is this happening? Who has the answers?

In the months since Hurricane Katrina, I have talked with so many people about the destruction witnessed on various news channels across the country. Friends and business associates from all over the nation have emailed or called to extend their sympathy and support, knowing I am from New Orleans. Nearly everyone has the same level of astonishment over what has taken place. Even those outside of our New Orleans and Gulf Coast area seem to grasp, to some degree, just how heart-wrenching this disaster has been. Concerts are being held to raise funds to help those in need, fundraisers all over the world continue to raise money for the displaced, sports teams are donating money, celebrities and politicians are calling for a response, FEMA and the Red Cross are offering much-needed assistance, and the church is rallying its troops. Those of us living through the madness are doing what we can for others while attending to our own lives as well. So many are dealing with the stress of this event, the upheaval it has caused, and the added pressure of having to live within confines much different from those to which we are accustomed. Families are living on top of each other, cities nearby are still overcrowded due to the migration of the displaced, traffic in evacuee areas is at a crawl, nerves are shot, and the future is uncertain. Months later, many still do not know where family members and friends are. It is still quite overwhelming.

So, how do we make any sense of this historic calamity? In the midst of our life's soul storm, which feels like 9-11 and the tsunami disasters wrapped into one, how do we put such things into any kind of mental framework that addresses the big questions we all have? What can we learn from the events in our lives that shake us to the core of our being? What should we learn from these events? Does any of this fit into a coherent worldview? Is God in this somewhere, somehow? Is there any word from a "loving

God" in moments like these? Where do we go from here? These are critical questions we all face at times like these. I believe there are answers. The answers are not "easy," and the ramifications go well beyond the physical and monetary impact we see, hear, and read about.

Ultimately, the disasters we witness via television, and those we encounter in our own lives, call us as people to look much harder at what we believe and why we believe it. The consequences of our belief, decision making, and life pursuits are tangible and far-reaching. The impact of our actions, thoughts, and deeds extend beyond us as individuals into our community, our nation, and our world. Ultimately, catastrophe speaks to us internally as individuals, but also to us externally as a global community and as a nation here in America. The lessons are as far-reaching as the reach of the storms, and the messages of hope, newness, compassion, grace, and repentance must be heard.

Because the impact of such enormous difficulties affects us psychologically, spiritually, and emotionally, we must take time to process them and find perspective. Historically, here in America, we have experienced a number of events that have had a profound impact upon our national psyche: Oklahoma City, Columbine, 9-11, and recently Katrina, to name a few. We continue, seemingly with increasing frequency, to see images of disaster brought our way. The real question, I believe, is whether or not we have wrestled appropriately with the impact of these events. Katrina, and those events prior to her and those yet to come, and all the attendant pain and destruction, offer us an ongoing opportunity to evaluate our lives as individuals and as Americans. While many questions surface, I believe the most critical question in the midst of these disasters concerns us as a people. What should we be learning about ourselves, about ultimate reality, about life, and about God's dealing with humanity? This is where true restoration will be found if there is to be any "rebuilding" of our souls, our communities, and our nation.

So let's begin the process.

SOUL STORM

PART ONE

DISASTER AT HAND

I was walking along a path with two friends—the sun was setting—suddenly the sky turned blood red—I paused, feeling exhausted, and leaned on the fence—there was blood and tongues of fire above the blue-black fjord and the city—my friends walked on, and I stood there trembling with anxiety—and I sensed an infinite scream passing through nature.

—Edvard Munch on the inspiration for his
famous painting *The Scream*

Soul Storm

During the many hours, days, and weeks following Hurricane Katrina I have realized over and over again the extent of the storm within me. The emotional, psychological, and spiritual displacement comes in waves, at times like a storm surge. One minute I feel the surge of exhilaration coming from thoughts of new beginnings, and the next I feel the waves of fear and uncertainty mounting. The thoughts, emotions, and intellectual challenges are wide-ranging, and the spiritual exercises are challenging. The questions and implications for all of us hit on so many levels: politics, religion, race, psychology, science, justice, compassion, humaneness, love, and restoration. This disaster, like many other national disasters we have seen before, causes us to rethink how we as a people relate to one another, to nature, and to God.

We have to reconsider how we extend opportunity to the underprivileged, how we show compassion to our neighbors, how we prioritize our lives, how we accept and receive help from others, and how we relate to our Creator. In the pages ahead, it is my hope that some sense can be made of all of this so we can all begin to rebuild not only the physical comforts that surround our lives but, more important, the spiritual core that may have been shaken by Katrina's ravaging gusts. If we set out with a steely-eyed determination to build it all back better than ever, but neglect the spiritual quadrant of this storm, then we will have missed many important lessons.

My hunger is to know and share with others the surpassing greatness of the grace of God, which leads us to Himself. It is in God's love that we find ourselves and the restoration He aims to bring to each of our lives. It is the extravagance of God's love and the brilliance of His loving gaze that captures us and secures for us a lifelong passion to "know Him and enjoy Him forever," as we are told is our God-given purpose as His beloved children. In His love we find who we are and what He has for us.

I am also assured that there are moments when God reaches us with loving discipline. In His love and grace, He extends to us a wake-up call to shake us out of patterns and modes of operation that have us settling for less than His best for us. Depending upon the severity of our spiritual blindness, God raises the stakes at times. Like any good parent who wants to lead a child down the right path, God gives us many chances to get it right, but He must ultimately raise the stakes at certain moments to get our attention. Is Katrina one of those high-stakes calls from a loving God? I cannot say for sure, but if so, we had better be listening at this point. The severity of this current storm, whether sent by God, allowed by God, or directed by God, should be enough to cause us as individuals, communities, and a nation to pause and reflect upon where we have been and where we are headed.

I am well aware that too often bad things happen to good people for seemingly unjust reasons. It is also clear that unjust horror is imposed upon good folks, and they must deal with it and move on as best they can. Life is not always fair, as we have been told. Sometimes we are dealt a bad hand, and we either bluff our way out or we just fold. In a broken world, crazy things and scary things just happen. Perhaps Katrina is one of those "bad moments" in life that we just have to process, work through, and move beyond as best we can. We will look into this possibility as well as we chase the implications of this storm.

Scientists suggest that we see these kinds of events as a result of global warming. Those investigating the break of the levees are now suggesting that political corruption and neglect were to blame for the destruction. We must consider each of these possibilities. Scripturally, we are taught that as a result of the fall of mankind in the Garden of Eden the entire world is groaning in pain due to the rift between God and His creation. Was Katrina little more than one big earth pain? Maybe. We are also taught in scripture that evil plans are brought to fruition by the enemy of God. Satan does have an agenda of destruction. Even in those circumstances, however, the plan of God shines through, and His purposes are not thwarted. Is it possible that Katrina was birthed in the belly of God's archenemy? We will consider this possibility.

Whatever conclusions we arrive at or fail to find, one thing is clear already—Katrina has left a scar upon our cities, our nation, and our hearts. She must be dealt with, and we must have some understanding of where we go from here and how we get there. Whatever the cause or causes for the carnage we have seen, there are lessons to learn from it. Whether we blame God, nature, or our leaders, the lessons remain. The lessons are many, they are wide in scope, and they are vitally important to our personal, communal, and national future.

The economic impact of Katrina has hit us all in the pocketbook. The political turmoil that has been apparent in the aftermath of her fury begs many questions. The subject of race has been brought front and center once again on the national stage as thousands of impoverished blacks were left stranded in Katrina's floodwaters, and now, months after the storm, many remain displaced. Katrina has raised questions regarding class differences, social structure, and city planning.

The power of Katrina speaks volumes about our obsession with our selves and our selfish agendas as people, especially as an American people. The crushing brutality of Katrina begs us to deal with our understanding of compassion and care. The desperation of Katrina moves us to come to grips with the reality that no matter how many things we may own, there is a more basic need beyond what we can see, touch, and buy. The call of Katrina speaks volumes about the proper place and need for the church to be a vital presence in the life of our nation. The discipline of Katrina is directing us to a place of repentance. And the ultimate questions Katrina poses to us all concerning how we live must be wrestled with honestly and openly.

Amidst the hard questions Katrina raises, heard in the whisper of her winds, is her message of restoration, hope, and reconciliation. Riding upon the waters of Katrina is the clarion call to greater aspiration, accomplishment, and God-ordained risk-taking. Katrina has gotten our attention, and she is forcing us to take a long hard look at who we are, where we have been, and where we are going as "one nation under God."

A word of prayer is in order as we venture forward in our attempt to hear Katrina's message and as we seek to find the mind of God on this subject:

"God, give us understanding as we rebuild. Enable us in the end to find hope to rebuild from the inside up. That is our prayer. Amen."

Losing It All

The losses are all too real. Sitting in a coffee shop recently, I overheard two strangers talking about how Hurricane Katrina had changed their lives. One gentleman shared how he lost his teenage daughter in the floodwaters that came up so quickly and with such force that nothing could be done to save the girl. His loss is great. One woman shared with me the enormity of loss brought not only by Katrina but by the brutality of living in a world full of illness and broken relationships. This woman, who had gone through a divorce recently, lost all of her possessions to the waters of Katrina and then on the heels of these two calamities witnessed the death of a child. Couples who had saved for a lifetime to build their dream homes lost them in a few hours' time. Still others, who were living lives of survival from day to day, saw the little they had snatched away in an instant. With nowhere to call home, and with little hope for tomorrow, to many victims of Katrina the loss seems more than they can endure. Pain and loss swirl around as an unrelenting torrent.

Anyone who has visited New Orleans knows of the unique character of this jewel of a city. To many, it is America's most alluring travel destination. World-famous restaurants, world-class music, a receptive people, parties unending, and Mardi Gras make the Big Easy one of the most visited towns in our country every year. Before Katrina, the movie industry became allured with the city, set up shop, and New Orleans became known as "Hollywood

South." Any day of the week people could walk the streets and see movies being shot, or run into a movie star in a jazz club or coffee shop. Every day or night, residents and visitors could pick their activity—NBA basketball, NFL football, beat-bopping jazz, the symphony, Broadway shows, dancing, minor league baseball, the Audubon Zoo, City Park, the lakefront, the Yacht Club, the Contemporary Art Museum, the New Orleans Museum of Art, the Fairgrounds, Jazz Fest, antique shopping, and on and on.

The city had so much, but it's all gone now. It's all been lost. It will never be the same. Or will it? Is it all really lost? Are we done in like some mythic city lost beneath the waters of fate? Maybe, maybe not. Perhaps it depends upon our response.

Enduring the Pain

Erykah Badu, songwriter and musician, has suggested, "The wise healer endures the pain. Cry. Tears bring joy." My Starbucks coffee addiction (tall lattes are my cup) led me to that quote, as it was found on one of their cups. The words have meaning and echo truth we have heard before. The scriptures read, "Weeping may endure for a night, but joy comes in the morning" (Ps. 30:5 NKJV).

We are in a great deal of pain. We are crying many tears. It will take time, and much endurance, but just maybe, joy will come for us one glad morning in the future.

How do we get to that glad morning? What must we learn if we are to have any hope for a bright future amidst such present pain and despair? Is all lost, really? This last question is much deeper than we may recognize at first glance. The steps in moving from horror to healing first require that we understand the questions we ask and also that we ask the right questions. Perhaps the better question in this case is not so much, "Have we lost everything?" but rather, "Exactly what have we lost?" The difference, though subtle, is utterly significant.

All of us will at some point in our lives face the realities of despair and the potent power of deep pain. All of us will at some point ask the questions that are now being asked by so many in the Gulf Coast area. I have talked with so many people in the days since the storm. What people have said has ranged from heartfelt, gut-level sincerity to angry and cutting political or racial outbursts. Everyone has had something to say about the lost city of New Orleans—Jay Leno, David Letterman, Ted Koppel, Stone Philips, Katie Couric and Matt Lauer, Larry King, and a host of others. Some have joked about it, others have expressed their sympathy, others write checks, and still others come to visit and have something to say while they are here. But are they saying the right things? More important, perhaps, are they asking the right questions?

Some want to know why city, state, or federal leaders did not do more to prevent some of the destruction. Others are asking why the levees did not hold. Scholars, politicians, celebrities, local residents, preachers, policemen, the elderly, the young, the good, and the bad all have something to say or some question to ask regarding this mess.

Many questions need to be asked, and answers should and will come to the vital questions being raised. However, the fundamental questions for those living through the reality of losing so much reach beyond much of the debated issues surrounding this tragedy. These fundamental questions are the same core issues that each living and breathing human on the planet wrestles with at one point or another, and most of us wrestle with these critical questions many times in our lives. How do we understand loss? What is ultimate loss? And, what do we do when it seems that all is lost? These are the questions that I am hearing, though perhaps in different words, from those dealing with the ravages of Hurricane Katrina. These are the very questions I have asked a number of times in my life as I have dealt with the realities of living in a broken world.

One very successful lawyer friend said to me recently, "I am screwed (though he used a less politically correct adjective). Nearly 60 percent of my legal business comes from the area that was hit the hardest. I don't know what I'm going to do." So many others have asked, "What are we going to do?" Just plain and simple, heartfelt, bottom-line questions: "What now?" One question people ask me, one that we will deal with later in the book, is of primary importance: "Did God do this?" There are answers to these questions, and those answers have tremendous value and relevance for our lives. The answers, if responded to properly, offer us hope, and yes, joy, amidst disaster. Let's take a look at the answers.

Taking a Beating

You've likely already heard the following passage many times; however, the application is too fitting to pass up. On one occasion, Jesus was intent on making the point that life must be lived according to one very fundamental principle—constructing one's life upon reality, truth, and ultimate certainty. In order to make His point, He offered a word picture, a story with a moral. Here is the way He presented the story that day:

> "Everyone then who hears these words of mine and does them will be like a wise man who built his house on the rock. And the rain fell, and the floods came, and the winds blew and beat on that house, but it did not fall, because it had been founded on the rock. And everyone who hears these words of mine and does not do them will be like a foolish man who built his house on the sand. And the rain fell, and the floods came, and the winds blew and beat against that house, and it fell, and great was the fall of it." (Matt. 7:24-27)

What Jesus was so passionate about teaching those listening on that day, and those of us wise enough to consider His words today, is simply this: "You had better use some common sense and sound judgment when it comes to building your life." Jesus did not suggest that all saintly types would escape tough times. In fact, He told His listeners that what the scriptures say is true, "It rains on the just and the unjust" (Matt. 5:45). That is to say that no one escapes disaster in this life. Storms do and will come. We will all see them, every one of us. The difference in our future depends on how well our lives are constructed prior to and despite the storms that assail us from time to time. Some people endure the storms and become healers for others. Others are ravaged by the storms and turn to bitterness, addictions, and all kinds of destructive patterns. Many are crippled by the winds and waves and choose never to get up and try again. Some wait until the intensity of the squalls of life die down and then make every attempt to return to life as usual.

Storm preparations and evacuation plans can and do save lives. Spiritual preparation and soul-storm evacuation plans can keep a soul intact when life gets nuts. Those who build their lives upon principles that have endured from generation to generation weather the storms of life. In contrast, individuals who live from moment to moment looking for the next dollar, the next fix, the next thrill, the next date, the next meal, the next trip — these people don't weather the storms so well. When life gets difficult, and the pressure is on, one's true character comes through. When everything and everyone around a person gets snatched away by illness, death, loss of property, betrayal, infidelity, or any number of other misfortunes, all is not lost for the individual who has built upon a sound foundation. Great is the impact upon others when endurance, grace, poise, and character are demonstrated throughout the storms of life.

And so, for those who have lost so much here in this world, and yet managed to retain their souls, all is not lost. For the Big Easy and the Gulf Coast region, this could very well be the road to the promised land. It is not fantasy to suggest that this may, in fact, be our greatest opportunity to move on to bigger and better things than we could have dreamed just a short time ago. While it is normal to deal with grief, uncertainty, and fear about the future, we must press on toward what lies ahead. Those who give up, those who quit and walk away, and those who just want life as it used to be will miss out on the realities of a new life that is unfolding.

Much has been taken away from the city of New Orleans. I wonder, however, how willing we are as a people to rid ourselves of those spiritual things that we have seen bring destruction to so many lives in our city. Some of the very things our city prides itself on are vices that have shackled our residents and visitors for years. Have we realized through this disaster just how fragile our existence is? Are we aware enough at this point to look not just at the physical damage, but also inside ourselves? Is the present disaster enough to cause us to evaluate our lives from a new perspective? Would we be able to rejoice if those things that bring our city lower — drunkenness, sexual immorality, drug use, extortion, political corruption, poverty, intellectual neglect, racial tensions — were to be removed?

Are we yet at the point where we view this storm as a window to allow God's light into our souls? We can surely go back to life as it used to be, but is that good enough? It is time for all of us in this country to allow ourselves room to consider ourselves and our cities in a different way. It is time to plan and dream about rebuilding not only our cities but also our nation for a better way, both physically and spiritually.

The answer then to the critical question, "What have we lost?" depends upon one's perspective. Jesus said, "For what shall it profit a man, if he shall gain the whole world, and lose his own soul?" (Matt. 16:26 KJV). These very words were offered in the context of Jesus' comments regarding the journey of life and the worth of pressing on toward a higher calling while enduring the difficulties that everyone must face. He was saying, in essence: "If you lose everything of material value in this world and gain God, you win. If, however, you win all the spoils life has to offer and miss God, you lose."

Therefore, the first step toward rebuilding a life, a city, a nation, or a soul, is to recognize that when all appears lost, all is not lost. The apostle Paul wrote, "For me to live is Christ, and to die is gain" (Phil. 1:21 KJV). For followers of Christ, everything here on earth is temporary. The goal for us is to make knowing Him our greatest passion and chief end. Further, the ultimate goal for us as people of faith is to be faithful, finish well, and then to die and meet our Maker. Even the best day here on earth, no matter how good, can't compare to that day when we see our Creator face to face. The rubbish of this world cannot compare to the surpassing beauty of heaven prepared for those who know the Lord of all creation.

I would like to suggest to anyone dealing with any loss of any kind, and especially to those caught in the misery of Katrina's wrath, that all is not lost. Life is different after a major disaster, no doubt. If you have been stung by the pain of losing a family member to terminal cancer or any other such serious disease, you know what I am speaking of. Those who have watched a spouse turn from God and family, and move outside the boundaries of marriage to find intimacy, know the pain of which I write. Children who have witnessed a family torn apart by divorce know this pain. Dreamers who have pursued their goals for years only to watch them vanish forever have experienced the bitter taste of emotional and psychological failure. And those who have worked so hard to attain financial freedom only to see their worth disappear in a flash know all too well how dramatically a disaster can alter one's life.

Yes, life is different after disaster. But all is not lost. I can tell you personally, having experienced in my life each of the storms just listed, that God can bring beauty from the ashes (Isa. 61:3 KJV). Where desolation once existed, new life can take root. Where the scourge of destruction once dominated the landscape, compassion can rise up, and healing can begin. If we allow Him to do so, God can enlarge our hearts amidst the difficulty. Like the Six Million Dollar Man, we can be built better than before!

There is indeed hope amidst the rubble. To find that hope, we must not only be willing to endure the squalls, but we must also learn to rest in God's purposes for our good amidst the tempestuous winds and waves.

Donne In: Lessons from John Donne

John Donne (1572-1631) was, perhaps, the greatest writer in the grand lineage of the many great seventeenth-century scribes. Once a Roman Catholic, trained at Oxford, and eventually an ordained minister in the Anglican Church, he was a marvel with language. Not only a great preacher, he was also a heavenly magician with the pen. His use of words captures the soul like few in history. Donne's ability to put to paper what most of humanity can only feel somewhere deep within but not express is seemingly beyond our realm. His writings, though rarely matched, are the inspiration of many great poets and writers of prose.

The depth of psychological insight, drama, and emotion in his words lead us to the heavens and to a place of passion we did not know existed within us. He was a complex person, and his thoughts were deep and meaningful. They offer us much insight into our discussion on finding God amidst disaster. Two of his Holy Sonnets offer us the divine view of suffering, pain, and ultimate purpose. Donne deals with our battle for proper affections in this life and the temptation to settle for less than God has for us.

As we will see shortly, Donne actually prays for more battering that he might be made into God's image. He also demonstrates for us, in his famous sonnet on death, that even in what we so often view as ultimate disaster, God has the last word. So, let's take a look at what he has to say on this vital subject.

Sonnet 14
Batter my heart, three-personed God; for You
As yet but knock, breathe, shine, and seek to mend;
That I may rise, and stand, o'erthrow me, and bend
Your force, to break, blow, burn, and make me new.

Let's pause here to look at these first few lines. What is Donne saying? He is actually asking, beseeching, God, to batter him. New Orleans has recently been battered by one of the biggest storms in history. Would we have ever prayed for such a battering? What if we knew that such a battering of our lives, our souls, could bring salvation? Would we dare voice such a prayer?

Donne continues by reminding God that up to this point the Creator had only brought a knock, a breath (small, quiet wind), and some warm sunlight to lead him down the right path. According to Donne, this has not been sufficient to captivate his affections. What a contrast to the health, wealth, and prosperity "gospel" we hear so much today! Donne goes a step further and calls on God to overthrow him, to forcefully break, blow, and burn him in order that he might be made new.

Do you see any parallels to the force of Katrina upon our neighborhoods? How much forceful breaking of structures, blowing of winds, and burning of buildings have we witnessed of late? *It can make us new!* One of the greatest writers in history, a man of God, suggests that this is the road to newness of life.

> I, like an usurped town to another due,
> Labor to admit You, but oh! To no end;
> Reason, Your viceroy in me, me should defend,
> But is captived and proves weak or untrue.

In these lines, Donne is telling why this battle within him is so intense and his struggle so severe. He suggests that his soul is overrun by an enemy that holds him captive. Though Donne labors to "admit" God in his life, it does not come to fruition because his worldly passions get in the way. Reason, which should convince Donne of his need to offer all to God, does not even do the job. Though common sense should defend us against the snares of this world, we too often fall prey to the allures of sin. Sin is pleasurable for the moment (Heb. 11:25). The problem is that those moments become habits, and those habits become addictions, and those addictions become our destruction.

> Yet dearly I love You, and would be loved fain,
> But am betrothed unto Your enemy.
> Divorce me, untie, or break that knot again,
> Take me to You, imprison me, for I

> Except You enthrall me, never shall be free;
> Nor ever chaste, except You ravish me.

Donne is crying out to God with abandon about his dilemma. Though his love for God tugs him, he cannot escape the grip of worldly living because of his marriage to things that are at war against God's purposes. In New Orleans, and in America for that matter, we claim such piety. We suggest that we are a "Christian" nation. And yet, are we not betrothed to so much that is in opposition to God's agenda? Is not New Orleans married to its revenue derived from vices of all sorts, which lure the tourists into our community? Does New Orleans, with all its charm, personality, food, and music, need the filth to keep the city afloat?

All that Donne has written in this sonnet leads up to the crescendo of the last few lines. It is here that we see Donne's need of a soul disaster for God's purposes to take root. Donne cries out for the storm to come. In a stirring, emotional torrent Donne begs God to break the bonds of marriage to his former life. He cries out for the Lover of his soul to break the knot that ties him to a false love. Rather than freedom to love the harlot of sin, Donne now hungers for the imprisonment of being confined to God's plan. That imprisonment is indeed where true freedom is found.

His use of paradox in these last few lines is riveting. He shows the value of this divorce of soul in light of his being jailed in the love of God. The enthralling power of God, he urges, is the key to freedom. Again, he throws himself before his Maker in surrender of the old life, taking on a blessed future.

That brings us to the last line: "Nor ever chaste, except You ravish me." It's worth reading again, isn't it? "Chaste." "Ravish." The two terms could not be more opposite. Much debate and inquiry has been made of John Donne's use of these words in this sonnet. The language, in that day, would have been jolting to the reader. In keeping with his mastery of English, Donne was reaching for words that take the reader as far as possible in order to demonstrate just how severe our need of God's love really is.

We live in a culture where the chaste man or woman is ridiculed. In our city, the recklessness of sexual immorality runs wild. In our nation, the promotion of sexual freedom is destroying the fabric of family life. In this last line, Donne shocks the reader by calling on God to "ravish" his soul. Some scholars suggest that the original usage of the word conveyed rape. Rape, by definition, is a taking by force what is not given or offered. Donne is suggesting that our need of a relationship with God and our obedience to Him is so great that we ought to allow the full force of God's rapturous love to overtake us and make us chaste unto Him.

In Donne's view, God's radical and disastrous acts on our behalf become the very means of our salvation! Oh, that we would see this natural disaster on the Gulf Coast as a means by which the Creator of the universe finally wins our cities, our souls, and our nation.

Donne and the Disaster of Death

Sonnet 10

Death, be not proud, though some have called thee
Mighty and dreadful, for thou art not so;
For those whom thou think'st thou dost overthrow
Die not, poor Death, nor yet canst thou kill me.
From rest and sleep, which but thy pictures be,
Much pleasure, then from thee much more must flow,
And soonest our best men with thee do go,
Rest of their bones and soul's delivery.

Thou art slave to fate, chance, kings, and desperate men,
And dost with poison, war, and sickness dwell,
And poppy, or charms can make us sleep as well,
And better than thy stroke; why swell'st thou then?
One short sleep past, we wake eternally,
And Death shall be no more; Death, thou shalt die.

Death has been a very personal reality for many of us living through Hurricane Katrina. Months later, the death toll continues to rise as more bodies are discovered in attics, cars, streets, and unexpected places. The stench of death still waifs through the air of the city of New Orleans months after the storm. Anyone who watched the news coverage of Katrina during the days following the storm will never forget the scenes from the New Orleans convention center.

It was here that the media shot video footage of Ethel Freeman, the ninety-one-year-old woman who, after days of enduring brutal heat without food or water, gave up the fight and died sitting in her wheelchair. She was left there, covered with a blanket, for days. Death is personal, and Donne speaks directly to this foe in his sonnet. Donne's decision to dialogue with Death is his attempt to demonstrate just how deeply our souls are impacted by the passing of others and our consideration of our own death. What Donne is making clear in his writing here is a message for anyone who has gone through the disaster of death whether it be the death of a dream, a lover, a husband, wife, child, marriage, or city.

The essence of the sonnet is simply this: Death does not have the last word. Whatever we have lost in death is replaced in the life-giving breath of God. God is willing and able to raise up lost things no matter how long they have been asleep. The reality of losing homes, cars, finances, businesses, and a city should not blind us to the truth that God in His infinite love and creative power is able to bring us back from the dead, spiritually and otherwise.

Donne speaks to death directly and informs this last enemy that many things in life can push us to the grave. However, the personal foe of death is defeated in the very moment it assumes that its victory is sure. For, in death, God raises the believer to a life beyond anything experienced on this side of the grave. Death, for the follower of Christ, becomes the doorway to new life, a better life. In death, the worry, anticipation, and fear come to an end, as we never again have to consider the possibility of being ultimately defeated! Donne points his finger in the face of death and directs its attention to its own demise. Death, in the end, comes to an end. Death loses; we win.

And so we must remind ourselves, amidst so much death and

destruction, that the city we so love has given up the old life, and up from the rubble now comes the budding of new life, a new future. Will we rejoice in the opportunity to pursue a better day for New Orleans, the Gulf Coast, and our nation? Or will we, very much unlike Donne, cling to the grave clothes of the past. Will we have the courage, in the aftermath of the storm, to turn to a higher way?

Surely, we do not want life as usual, life as it always was. There is more than that. If you have confronted the many faces of death in your life, I would like to remind you that you are not done in. Whether you have seen the evils of the world in the form of violence, rape, molestation, emotional abuse, prison, adultery, or cancer, it is not over. You do not have to remain bitter, numb, and overwhelmed. God is not through with you yet. Look up! New life is on the way. The Lover of your soul, the One who has ordered the time of your passing, is calling to you to embrace a life beyond anything you could have imagined. Run to Him for shelter from the storm.

Choosing Death over Life as Usual

As a people, a city, and a nation, we need to consider the possibility that there are things we must die to. In dying to things that hinder us from attaining all that life offers, we are in actuality embracing life in all its fullness. This paradox should not shock us. Accomplishing anything always entails giving something up. Doctors must spend years and years devoting themselves to nothing but study in order to prepare for the valuable work they do. Professional athletes must begin very early in life devoting many hours, days, and years to nothing but their training. A retirement nest egg, unless acquired by winning the lottery, is built up by a disciplined storing away of a part of one's earnings decade after decade.

Spiritual growth takes place only as we put aside—die to— those things that hinder our spiritual development. In God's plan, death, though associated with pain, is the beginning of a better life. God indeed calls us to die to certain things throughout our lives in order that He might accomplish His plans. He also calls nations to die to certain things in order that He might remain with a people, bless them, and carry out His plan through them. The Creator does this, not because He is opposed to our experiencing pleasure, but rather because He knows all and sees the consequences of our actions as a people. God's call for any person or people to die is a call to embrace peace, joy, fulfillment, significance, and meaning. To turn a deaf ear to God's call for purity, moral character, absolute truth, and holiness is to ignore His forecast of impending doom.

Our world is broken as a result of our earliest ancestors ignoring the most trustworthy forecaster ever to predict a storm. The book of Genesis reminds us of this truth. After creating us in His image, God gave us a blueprint for life and a warning about stepping outside of the blueprint. Genesis 2:15-17 reads, "The LORD God took the man and put him in the garden of Eden to work it and keep it. And the LORD God commanded the man, saying, 'You may surely eat of every tree of the garden, but of the tree of the knowledge of good and evil you shall not eat, for in the day that you eat of it you shall surely die.'"

God created mankind with a free will in order that His creation might have a choice to follow Him. Love of God is a choice, a daily choice. To turn away from God's plan is to choose to remain within the walls of a shabbily built house with a shaky foundation and a Category-Five storm on the way. As we have all seen, that's not a good plan. The One who loves us, created us, and has our best interest in mind wants to protect us from a life of emptiness and godless sorrow.

And so, the admonition is to choose and to choose wisely. Every individual has many moments in life where critical decisions must be made, decisions that will have an impact for years to come. Some of these decisions will impact life from here to the grave. Many people, and indeed the residents of the city of New Orleans and the citizens of this nation as a whole, have reached a decision-making moment. In the shocking aftermath of what we have just seen, the time has come for a deep soul searching.

As a "nation under God," we must make a conscious choice, a vital choice. How will we rebuild this place? Who will be our builder? Who will be the architect? The only way to move forward to a secure future is to choose the one and only faultless architect the world has ever known. Should New Orleans choose to build on the same foundation that existed before, the consequences could be severe. There is a better way to build our city and our nation. At this crossroads, just as is true at any critical juncture in life, the wisdom of God must be employed. If we are to construct physical, moral, and spiritual levees that will hold in the future, we must give greater thought to the blueprint given to us in the scriptures.

We must die to those things that bring death to our city and nation and open our hearts to a new way. Colossians 3:5-6 reads: "Put to death therefore what is earthly in you: sexual immorality, impurity, passion, evil desire, and covetousness, which is idolatry. On account of these the wrath of God is coming." As we put aside that which has brought death into our city and our nation in the form of poverty, racial tensions, murder, political corruption, injustice, and immorality, God will grant us peace, stability, value, hope, and a future. Though the pursuit of unbridled passions is championed in our society through various media on a non-stop basis, the reality is that living for self and for pleasure leads to destruction: "For the wages of sin is death, . . ." (Rom. 6:23) we are told in scripture. We see this fact played out on the news twenty-four hours a day. In contrast, God offers us life: ". . . but the free gift of God is eternal life" the verse continues.

Disasters of any kind present us with opportunity to reassess who we are and what our lives are about. Our country has had many moments to pause and consider our foundations in recent years, and they all remind us that the foundations of our lives must be stable if we are to remain strong. Our future depends upon our spiritual structure. The future of our cities, our country, and our world depends upon how we design our lives and who we choose as our designer.

Disaster as a Turning Point: A Tribute to Mamaw

The bend in the road is not the end of the road, unless you refuse to make the turn.

—Anonymous

January 13, 2005, was a turning point, a critical moment. On that date I had to deal with a significant disaster in my life. This disaster came at a time when all around me was chaos, uncertainty, and pain. I was going through major transitions in my family, finances, and the call of God for my future. All the difficulties had been in place for some time, and the level of stress was enormous at the start of a new year. Yet somehow, I knew deep within me that in the midst of this storm God was at work. January 13, 2005, was to be a day in which all the elements of the storm would come to a head, and the beginning of a new day of hope would begin for me.

"Unlucky thirteen" was to be a day of death in my family. "Mamaw," the matriarch of our family, passed away and went on to be with her Maker. In her passing, I found pain and sorrow, but also perspective. Mamaw's passing was not a shock to anyone in our family, and we were all about as "prepared" as we could be for her last day. She had been diagnosed with cancer three years earlier, and was told she had only six months to live.

We all expected this day would come many months earlier than it did. But as Mamaw was prone to do on such occasions, she thanked the doctors for their diagnosis, looked them squarely in the eyes, and told them and us that she was in God's hands and that she suspected she would be around a bit longer that anyone might assume. She proved herself and her God right, once again. Mildred Findley was never one to place more faith in the wisdom of this world than in the truths she read in the scriptures every day. The many Bibles she had in her home were a demonstration of her source of trust. Each of them, of which I now have the last one she had been poring through, are a visible reminder of how she devoured the words of God, for they are full of notes, paper clips, and highlights.

Mamaw was not an accomplished academic, she was not a world traveler, she was not well known, she was not rich, and her contributions to life on this planet were not visible to most of the world. However, she lived a life of love and devotion to God and His call to grace and compassion. Mamaw rarely traveled more than a couple hundred miles from her home. She was a simple woman prone to state things in a heartfelt country tone. While none of her daily sermons, anecdotes, or directives was recorded for posterity, her teachings are alive and well in the hearts of all of those who had the privilege of knowing her. To know Mamaw was to be loved, deeply.

Though I loved my grandmother a great deal, and though I knew who and what she was about, the full impact of just how important her contribution in my life was did not come until I had to prepare for her funeral. As I reflected upon this simple but profound life, I came to realize just how God used her to form me over the years. In my preparations for the sermon, I wept many tears, but not just tears of sorrow. The tears were coming from the great loss, yes, but also from the deep sense of gratitude to have had the blessing of God to grow up around this woman. Her life, I was now understanding in ways I had not before, had given me the foundation to withstand many of the intense tempests that have come my way. Mamaw's life and death, a turning point for all who knew her, left a mark on me. Her legacy will live on.

What was this life about? What lasting good can really come from such a simple existence? Mildred Findley's life was a humble one, but it was a life well lived, and that's the point. All of us want to know that our lives mean something, don't we? I have heard it said that what a life really amounts to is not the dates on the tombstone, but the dash in between. The dates are on Mamaw's tombstone, yet it is the dash that speaks so much to all of us who loved her.

That dash was filled with grace amidst struggle, compassion amidst sickness, care for scraped knees, a cold washcloth on the forehead on sick days, big buckets of bubble gum, and tons of loving words. Mildred was a woman acquainted with the disasters of this world, and yet she did not find herself consumed with her own pain. Throughout this well-lived life, she gave of herself to others with abandon. She cared for the elderly with unceasing compassion, she showed great love to the many she cared for as they struggled with terminal illness, and she always, without reservation, pointed the sufferer's gaze upward to a compassionate God. Time spent in Mamaw's presence was always restoring. No one who showed up at her house needed an invitation, and all were welcome. To know Mamaw was to know you were loved, loved for just showing up.

I will never forget the trips to the nursing homes when she would take me there to see Granny Findley. The huge Christmas and Thanksgiving celebrations that were so full of food, fun, and family, and the countless days she cared for me and fought for me remain in my soul. The sleepless nights she spent for months on end caring for Papaw when he was nearing his end, and the nights she stayed up with my mother as my stepfather lost the battle with cancer at the age of only twenty-seven are etched in my soul as well.

In the days leading up to January 13, 2005, our family kept an around-the-clock vigil. Mamaw was coherent and involved with us until the last day or two. It was staggering to see the peace, contentment, and certainty about her future that she demonstrated all the way through. Though we were there to comfort her, she was really the one comforting us. It was surreal. I think she hung on until she absolutely knew we were ready to move on even as she passed on to bigger and better things above. Literally, until the last day here on earth, she was full of grins, handing out treats to the kids (oh, that bubble gum!), and having all of us climb up in the bed next to her so she could love on us.

"Amazing love, how can it be?" I watched as she took her last breath. I held her in my arms and whispered to her that it was all right for her to move on. And as I sit here writing these words with tears in my eyes, I can vividly remember those tangible moments. In those moments, ripe with the sweetness of God's touch, I came to understand how living a life of value along the dash contributes to one's ability to move on when all around is loss. In God's scheme, loss is designed for a certain time, place, and purpose. Mamaw lived her life according to that design, she lived and loved like she knew where she was going, and she left a legacy for all of us to follow.

My life was so full of difficulty even as I lay beside her in those last moments. And as I whispered to her that everything would be right, she was still thinking about me, and whispered back, "I love you. I am ready. You will be fine. God is going to give you a new start." As Mamaw stepped across the neck of the enemy into God's arms, she was still encouraging, loving, and leading the way for others. My life and my future are richer because of her extravagant love for others, which came from the matchless love of God shining in her soul. The strength of force of God's call on my life was renewed as I watched my grandmother deal Death his final blow. She went out swinging and went upward with grace. Her courage in the face of disaster, her peace amidst the storm, her love throughout years of kingdom battles give me the strength to overcome the challenges life sends my way.

Reflection upon her life has stirred me to remember that life is not about fame, money, power, success, travel, and pleasure. Life is about loving and impacting others for God's agenda. In the days since her death, God has lifted me and sent me in new directions with renewed passion for His purposes.

As Mamaw lay dying on the bed in my aunt and uncle's home in Slidell, Louisiana (one of the many homes flooded by the waters of Katrina), the whisper of God came to me in a tangible way. It was as if I could hear the soft whisper of God telling me, "In this loss, Bruce, is the start of a new day." This is a message that is true for all of us. Whether you have had the privilege to have a Mamaw in your life or not, God's love reaches out to you in ways much like my grandmother's love reached out to me. He is faithful to send whispers of His grace if we are listening for His voice. Those whispers often come at unexpected and unassuming moments, but they do come.

The God of the universe longs to make Himself known to you amidst all the seasons of your life. I recognize that all too many people in our world are without the kind of loving support I found in my grandmother. You may be one of those people. God is able, however, to give you strength and a network of loving and supporting people. Some have seen families disintegrate amidst the pain of broken relationships, others have lost close family members to illness, still others have seen those they love move away to pursue the goals given to us by a mobile society chasing the all-alluring American dream.

Whether the network of loving relationships and deep friendships has been there or not up to this point in your life, God stands ready and willing to bring you to a new day. If all appears lost for you, if you have given up hope of being loved or giving love, God can and will provide an answer for you, if you will take him up on it. In the restoration of family relationships or through an authentic and open church community, God is able to meet you. If we will take the time to allow God to speak to us, even the worst of disasters are the means by which our God will move us on to greater things. No matter how strong the winds, no matter how deep the waters, no matter how severe the destruction, amidst all the storms of life God can bring newness, a hope, and a future.

"I Have Plans for You": My Personal Disaster Story

For I know the plans I have for you, declares the LORD, plans for wholeness and not for evil, to give you a future and a hope. (Jer. 29:11)

"Help us!" "Someone, please, respond." "Come get us." These were but a few of the signs seen on CNN as those trapped by the waters of Katrina cried out for help. What a desperate scene it was to watch. More desperate, no doubt, to be the one on the roof. My stepfather and his elderly mother wound up on one of those roofs, trapped in St. Bernard Parish, one of the hardest hit areas in New Orleans.

What do we do when we need help and answers, and wonder if anyone is there to respond? How do we make sense of the crisis? Does anyone have a plan?

I was born in Baton Rouge in 1968. My mother, after watching her husband, my father, make some very bad decisions that brought much pain into her life, decided to pursue a divorce when I was two years old. From that time, with the exception of a few narrow windows of time, I saw very little of my father. I grew up in a home with my mother, and often my grandmother, where nurturing and encouraging words overcame much of what I would miss by not having a father. My grandfather's presence and care was of great help along the way also. Struggling with the lack of relationship with a dad was never an issue for me even when times were the darkest. Looking back, I have come to understand that the reason I felt so secure in a "broken" home was due to the knowledge that I was loved deeply by those around me. I never struggled with esteem issues or insecurity. Knowing I was loved at home gave me strength when the storms of life sent pelting rain into my soul as a young person.

My father and nearly everyone on his side of the family were gifted athletes. My dad was a strong baseball player and a great golfer as were his brother and father. His brother was actually one of the best quarterbacks to go through Bogalusa High School. Those genes were passed on to me. What I did not get were my grandfather's height genes. That twist of genetic fate would set the stage for years of frustrated aspiration and unfulfilled dreams.

Growing up in a home with a single working mom had its advantages for a kid who loved athletics. Because my mother was working to support us, I needed a place to be for hours on end. That was fine with me because I loved being in any and every athletic venue. I seemed to always feel a little bit like Eric Liddell, the gifted runner and missionary, who when defending his love of running and his Olympic dream to his sister who wanted him to leave the running for the mission field, said, "God has made me for a purpose. But He has also made me to run, and when I run I feel His pleasure." For me, to compete, to use the body and ability God had given me, was to feel alive.

To this day I love to compete, and when I do, I compete with all that is within me. I just think, whatever we do, ought to be done with all that is within us. If we are going to do it, we should be passionate, and leave a mark. Watching the best of Michael Jordan's days, Walter Peyton's finest runs, John McEnroe's highlight reels, or an Ozzie Smith acrobatic play at shortstop is like watching a live work of art or ballet.

As much as I loved athletics growing up, I could not get everything I wanted out of it as early as I wanted to. I was hindered from developing to my full potential as a tennis player or a baseball player by a couple of things. First of all, my mother, though she gave all she could and more, could not afford the high-priced training camps and boarding schools where the best of the best got the edge up in training. The bigger hindrance, however, was my height, or lack thereof. That was a hindrance not only because of size, but also because when all things were even, typically the bigger athlete was given the nod. There was never a coach I played for who did not say I was the hardest worker. I was always told I had the best attitude and work ethic. Many, if not most, would even suggest that I had the most talent.

One coach along the way, formerly an Olympic trainer, suggested to me and an entire team that the performance I had just demonstrated was the greatest display of athleticism he had ever seen on any level. That was heady and inflating, but also frustrating at the same time. It was frustrating because I knew the clock was ticking, and I had not seen the growth spurt that touched all other good athletes. I knew that without that extra six inches, I would not get a top college scout to even look at me.

According to the endocrinologists, the problem was that "something" was missing. In order for me to have any hope of catching up with the growth curve in time and pursuing a big tennis scholarship, I would have to have growth-hormone injections. When the day came that I was told that something was missing and it could be fixed, I was elated—I had hope! But just before I was to begin taking the scheduled injections, some research came out calling into question the safety of the injections. The "help" was then snatched away by the FDA. That period in my late teenage years was a tough one. My mother, my grandmother, and I cried many tears during that time. No one else, with perhaps one or two exceptions, even knew this storm was raging within me.

Not to be deterred, I dug in my heels and trained even harder on the tennis court. Though I had always loved baseball, in my later teenage years, tennis became my deepest passion. I would start practicing at 8:00 a.m. and go all the way through 6:00 p.m., seven days a week. When I was not on the court, I was jumping rope thousands of times, working out, or running around the football stadium in City Park. If you have seen the video footage of the Hurricane Katrina disaster, you may have noticed this stadium, all but the top level, beneath the floodwaters in New Orleans. That scene brought back so many years of memories.

By the time I was seventeen, and a senior in high school, I decided college tennis was what I really wanted to pursue. Because I dedicated myself to the game later than usual, I knew I needed one more year to train very hard if I was to get a scholarship at a major tennis school. When I graduated from Brother Martin High School in New Orleans, I took a year off to train and work toward that scholarship I wanted. Making great progress, at least in my view, I thought I was on my way.

Then more pain set in, this time in the form of a major back injury. While playing in a tournament at City Park, I backpedaled to hit an overhead, jumped in the air, and came down off balance with the full weight of my body landing directly on my lower back. I was stunned and in pain, but I continued with the match and finished out the tournament the next day. Over the course of the next month, the pain in my back became more and more severe. Eventually, a training program that typically lasted five to seven hours per day had to be cut off after only an hour. The pain left me unable to even get to the car some days.

After many doctors' visits and multiple X-rays, the problem was found. A congenital condition leaving the fifth lower lumbar off kilter was to blame for the pain. The condition is typically non-symptomatic unless a major trauma activates it, usually in the form of a car accident, but in my case, a sports injury. The fix? Surgery. My answer? "No thanks!" I had known too many people who were ruined by bad back surgery, and I had watched enough suffering in hospitals to know that was a place I did not want to be. Just a few years earlier I had watched my stepfather (who was the first to introduce me to the game of tennis) at the age of twenty-six go in to the hospital for a back ache, come out diagnosed with cancer, and die a year later. I gave up my training schedule and my goal. A dream died, and my soul felt a deep pain.

At this point I began to review my life. I looked back over the years and recalled the moments of inspiration, the dreams, the hopes, and I felt like they had all been dashed. I recalled the joy my mother had experienced when she found a new love in Don, my stepfather, gave birth to my wonderful sister Michelle, and watched that love get cut short when my sister was but three years old. I remembered all the hours of prayer at Lakeview Christian Center in New Orleans (another place rich with memories lost in the waters of Katrina) and the prophetic words of healing called out for Don. Confusion over why God would give someone athletic ability only to shorten the dream stirred in my soul like a tornado. Thinking about life and its meaning had not been a priority for me until this point.

It was about this time that I went on a couple of life-changing mission trips in third-world countries. Those trips changed my perspective. God began to arrest my heart as I watched people with real problems try to find a hope and a future. God had laid the groundwork for transformation years before in the example of many godly men in our church. These men had lived the Christian life in front of me with authenticity and grace for many years, and I had the sense along the way that these men—who loved sports, were successful, and "normal"—really had something I was missing.

On the mission field, amidst my own soul storm, with the lives of these men as the backdrop for my understanding of God, the Lover of my soul began to "batter" my heart. My eyes moved from my own pitiful condition to the condition of others, and the agenda of God became my new focus. Those early days of faith were full of passion, hunger, and thirst for all I could take in of God and His Word. It was like a new romance. And I pursued it, with a passion.

During that time I was attending the University of New Orleans and finding no desire for any of the studies in business I was pursuing. After three semesters there, I had the unquestioning sense that God was calling me to theological education. I left the University of New Orleans, left my city, left my family, and cried like a baby for about two weeks! That decision, however, was crucial in many ways.

At the time I was leaving, an interesting thing had developed. Over the course of a year and a half, my passion for God had not grown cold, and yet I found myself struggling intensely with doubts about the reality of God, His existence, and His purposes for our lives. I still remember the week before I left. Sitting on a ski lift in Telluride, Colorado, with a mentor and surrogate father, Bill Treeby, I told this large, silver-haired senior attorney and church elder of my dilemma. Here I was, going off to theology school doubting the very existence of the One I was going to study.

What in the world was going on? We talked it through and prayed, and I left with a sense that God would move on my behalf. More than anything, though, I knew a trusted friend had heard me out, understood, and believed in me. Bill and Nancy Treeby, though we may not have agreed on everything or seen everything eye to eye along the way, cared for me more than anyone outside of my family through the years. I am forever grateful for them, and my life has been made much richer because of them. They embraced me when I had lost my second father, Don, to cancer, and counted me as one of their own, taking me on ski trips, buying me meals, and providing for me in more ways than I can recount here.

God did, indeed, meet me in my doubts. Upon arriving at the Christian school for my undergraduate work, Southeastern College in Lakeland, Florida, I found God's loving hand displayed to me in a very tangible way. I have not had many of these moments in my Christian life, but this was one of those you never forget. My questions had become so troubling that I felt plagued by doubts. "Plagued" was, in fact, the very word I would use when crying out to God about the struggle. On the first day of class, with a professor whom I had never met, God spoke directly to my doubts. The professor began that first class with prayer. Right in the middle of praying, he stopped and said that he felt as if God were directing him to pray for someone who recently had been "plagued by doubt." My mouth hit the floor, my eyes poured seas of tears, and my heart leaped toward God in thankfulness.

It was in those days at Southeastern that God really began to birth in me a deep and abiding call to serve Him. Early on, the fire in me was to be used by God to call the church to be what she ought to be, can be, and is called by God to be. As elating a feeling as that was, and is, I did not know the pain that would be associated with it. I made the "mistake" of asking God to develop me for His purposes no matter what the training program might entail. That's a dangerous way to pray. He always takes us up on that kind of sincere prayer, so beware.

Academically, socially, and spiritually, I did well at Southeastern. I loved the academic pursuit, and studied very hard. Teaching and preaching appealed to me, and I had a sense that

God would use me in those arenas. I was often asked to preach or teach at school, at churches in which I served, and at youth-group meetings, and the administration honored me by selecting me to be the commencement speaker for graduation ceremonies.

Albeit on a smaller level, I did get to play college tennis, and was named MVP all four years. One sweet extension of God's extravagant love during those college tennis days was a moment in which I was allowed to hold the French Open trophy that had just been won by Jim Courier. It was as if God were sending one of those cool whispers of His grace, saying, "You may not have gotten there, but I am aware, and I have better plans." Not many people who love and play the game, no matter how good they are, get to see, let alone hold, a real Grand Slam trophy. Along the way, I had met my future wife and colaborer in the ministry, and we had two children while still in school. It all looked so picture perfect.

We had started "adult life" early, my wife and I. After meeting at the college we were both attending, with spring in the air and fairy tale ideas of what life in ministry would be like, we dove in headfirst. I was twenty-one, and my bride was nineteen. After a less than Princess Di and Prince Charles-styled wedding, we set off to the mountains in Telluride for a blissful honeymoon, and soon returned to Lakeland to begin our quest for heroic feats in the church. The idea was to watch God bring two people together from broken homes, restore what had been taken from them, heal their deep hurts, and use that couple to win the world to Christ. Three months into the marriage, we were looking forward to the birth of our first child, and sixteen months later, we were redecorating for our expected second addition. During that time, I was in school full time, studying a second major, working in a church, and holding down a part-time pizza delivery job. We hit the ground running at a grueling pace, but it was "all for the kingdom."

The fairy tale seemed to be in place, but then ministry happened. I have done a number of things in my life professionally now, and have come to appreciate and believe what others told me long ago: Ministry is the toughest road one could ever take. As a lay person, it can seem like the ministers in the church read, pray, talk, encourage, and live a heroic life leading others to God. What could be better than that? In reality, a minister's life looks and feels much different from the inside. Always on call, surviving on very limited funds, striving to meet expectations beyond any reality, and displaying high-octane performance required on demand—all of this leads to high stress and a very high burnout rate. And that's if everything goes really well!

In our case, we soon saw the dark side of the church. Friedrich Nietzsche, who is infamous for being involved with the "death of God" movement decades ago, commented that he would be more prone to believe in the Christ of Christianity if Christians acted a bit more like the Christ they proclaimed. I came to understand that sentiment early in my journey.

From my vantage point in ministry, it seemed that churchgoers, and particularly those involved in church leadership, were all too prone to speak one way and live another. There were moments when I saw such hypocrisy that it turned my stomach. At times I watched as the church pleaded for money, for "survival," while the leadership was driving luxury automobiles. I watched as nepotism, rather than the call of God, seemed to be the formula for ministry opportunity. I saw churches where praise and worship was nothing more than an emotional pep rally on the verge of charismatic manipulation, and I painstakingly endured other "worship" settings where Mr. Rogers would have been viewed as a hyperactive chandelier-swinging lunatic.

Churches without life raise questions regarding the validity of faith just as much as unbiblical and "irrational exuberance." My wife and I saw the church use resources in ways that made us question what was really going on. At one point, we were in school, working jobs, raising kids, ministering in the church, and being forced to live on food stamps and Medicaid. One would think that the church would always care for those within the fold, certainly its leaders.

All of this led to a storm so intense it is hard to describe. I wondered if God were ever really in my aspirations for ministry, if He really had a plan, and if He really knew of my tears. My wife struggled with bitterness, doubt, and deep pains that eventually led to total emotional breakdown.

After graduating from college with a double major in preaching and pastoral ministry, and after having served in one church that overall was very refreshing and uplifting, I thought God had opened the windows of heaven and heard my cry. My time serving with a young, vibrant, and progressive pastor in a growing church in Lakeland, though rewarding, came to an end as my aim had grown to further my theological education. I applied to graduate schools, got my first choice, and was accepted at Wheaton Graduate School outside of Chicago. Yes, that's the place that claims Billy Graham as it most notable product. At that point in my life, it seemed like the Promised Land to me. I was off to pursue a master's degree at a renowned graduate school. School was great; ministry and home life were not so great.

In order to sustain the family while I was in school, I took a position in a church that did not provide the environment I expected. Initially, I thought I was walking into a ministry position to help build a youth group from the ground up in an Evangelical setting. It did not take long to figure out that I was out of my element. After several months of struggle, it became clear that not only were my family and I not being fed spiritually, we are also being asked to stop teaching the Bible as absolute truth and Jesus as the only way to salvation. I had come face to face with a reality I would learn much more about in my graduate education — mainline churches in America were abandoning the historic fundamentals of faith and losing their power to transform lives.

I had not signed on in ministry to do day care for teens; I wanted to see lives changed. Seeing the church in this light was another blow for my wife. For her, it was yet another example of why ministry was just not where she felt most at home. She had always questioned my decision to take the position at the church, and the stress of the situation was taking its toll on both of us. She began to wholeheartedly look outside the church to use her talents and gifts in the arts.

During this time, one saving grace was our proximity to Willow Creek Community Church in Barrington, Illinois. We attended regularly, and loved it. While at Wheaton, my study program was a focus on the church in America. In my studies, I was given a fascinating look at the development of the church in this country historically, sociologically, and theologically. I had come to some conclusions about the future of the church in the United States and beyond, and I strongly suspected that Willow Creek's model would be a strategic model for the expansion and impact of the church.

God began to birth in me a passion to build a church along the Willow model that would reach people with a creative, artistic, intelligent, and authentic presentation of the Gospel. I just knew at that time, this would be my future. Everything I had seen, experienced, and suffered through in the various churches over the years was leading up to the moment when God was going to put me in a place of leadership in a vibrant church like Willow.

Just as I was thinking along these lines, my wife was having a great time at the Art Institute of Chicago, one of the world's best art schools. After she had attended there for a short time, one of her professors gave her the opportunity to do some design work in her home, which quickly evolved into a fast-paced business. For me, the stresses were mounting at home with travel to school every day, two kids, my wife's job, and my study load, so we dropped back to punt. I had finished my course work and needed only my thesis project to complete my degree, but in light of the pace and stress, I gave up the thesis research and prayed for God to provide that leadership spot I coveted in a cutting-edge church. It looked like it was going to happen.

Through a series of events I found myself in the hunt for the lead pastoral position in a church so much like what I wanted that I was salivating. Everything seemed to fit so well from my viewpoint. Surely, I thought, this was going to be the place where God was going to prove the reasons for all of the madness we had seen in ministry in the past. It was all going to make sense now. This was the payoff for all of the financial, emotional, and relational sacrifice.

After I had gone through several interviews over the phone and in airports, the search team gave me half a nod. They suggested that they were 90 percent sure I was the man they were looking for. The only glitch was that one more candidate had just surfaced at the end of the timeline they had set for themselves. They went on to tell me that our qualifications, style, backgrounds, and gifts were similar, but they just wanted to make sure they had followed due diligence in the selection process. I thought it would be no big deal, as I had just won the race over a slew of others God had not commissioned for this task that was to be mine. I wanted this job badly, and God wanted it for me, I was certain. Then I got the call. The search team had chosen the other candidate. Equals, they said, but they just decided to go with the other guy.

That was one of the darkest days I had experienced in my Christian walk. In fact, it was the darkest to that point. This just did not make sense, I thought. I had given so much. My wife and I had given up so much, endured so much, prayed so much, and struggled so much. "Why?" a million times, "Why?" we asked. The answer just did not come.

We decided to take a break from the ministry. So we moved to downtown Chicago and began to focus on the design business. We still attended Willow, and loved it, and occasionally dreamed about doing church "the right way," but the business took off, and the fun of the city was a reprieve. The fun lasted there for awhile. Our beautiful kids were growing older. They got into modeling in the city, and did very well. We ate out, went to the zoo, walked the Magnificent Mile, toured the museums, spent pockets full of money at Niketown, and appreciated life from a different perspective.

That lasted for some time, but eventually the pace and stress of big-city life caught up with us. In the big city, you work on demand, twenty-four hours a day, seven days a week, or you don't get the contract. My wife was spending long hours working very hard, I was struggling to find a really viable job outside of our design business, and emotionally we were spent. We did not see enough of each other or our kids. Willow Creek had remained our source of strength and spiritual growth, and ultimately we decided it must be time to move back to my hometown and start a Willow model church from the ground up.

We set off with renewed visions of greatness and dreamed of what God might do. I was more convinced of the decision than my wife, I would later come to realize. She left part of herself back in Chicago and resented not having finished her education at the art school, but I was not, in my mind, fulfilling God's call for me there. It was a tough mix. Not too long after we arrived back home, a series of financial, relational, and strategic missteps led to another disaster. This time, I had not just lost a ministry opportunity or a thesis; rather, it appeared I was losing a wife.

Not too long before this situation developed, I could not have imagined my life getting any harder, but at this juncture it did. I walked through the darkest days of my life, to that point, finding out that I was no longer the sole love of my wife's life. The depth of pain was beyond anything I could have ever imagined. The grief literally felt as if it were going to kill me at times. I shed tears, I lost weight, and I questioned who I was and where I was going. What a disaster.

God showed up in the midst of that pain. He extended His grace to me and to my wife and led us on a road to reconciliation. The pain, as deep as it had been, was replaced by a sweetness and a depth in our relationship that had not been there before. We grew as Christians, as a couple, and as a family. Eventually, we were blessed with a new source of grace from God, a daughter, Isabella Grace, so named for the beauty of God's grace. From the embers of destruction, God brings wonderful things. God also provided financially in ways we had never experienced. His provision enabled us to overcome financial obstacles, travel the country and beyond, and provide a great life for our kids. It was a refreshing time.

That time of refreshing proved to be the eye of the storm. It was a fairly large eye, but just an eye nonetheless. Several years after this time of renewal and reconciliation had begun, the winds of a tempest would begin to blow once again. This time the winds and the rain were too much. As severe and damaging as the front side of the storm had been, in this storm, its greatest wrath was to be found at its rear. The development of this catastrophic storm was years, if not decades, in the making. All the combined environmental and stratospheric elements had come together for what would be the flattening of a marriage.

Bitterness, the tug of worldly affections, the pull of success outside of home and family, and a desire for something that only God could give had grown like a toxic mold and taken over, and I witnessed a second betrayal. The assessment of details, weather patterns, preparedness, and forecasting are all convoluted in this storm's aftermath. The cleanup and rebuilding effort for the souls involved will take years, perhaps lifetimes. God says He hates divorce, and I know why—it crushes souls. It crushes the souls of men, women, boys, girls, and onlookers. It is a storm from which individuals ought to run for cover. This is a storm to be avoided at all costs. Its floodwaters rise too high and too fast, and its storm surge rips hearts from their foundations. Beware this storm!

The storm, however, does not have the last word! There is yet hope. God is able to sustain. Newness does spring forth. Eventually, the waters do recede, the debris is removed, and the sound of hammers and saws is heard again. In God's economy, the damage is never irreparable. As deep as the waters have been, God's grace has been deeper. As strong as the winds have been, God's whisper has been stronger. As piercing as the pain has been, the comfort of God has been so much more tender. And as uncertain as the future has seemed at times, how much more steadfast has been the matchless love of God! Never has there been a storm that He could not quiet. Never has there been a life He could not rebuild. Never has there been a soul He could not redeem and restore. This book, I hope and pray, is a testimony to that fact. God is rebuilding me even as I write. I still believe in the plan. Thanks be to God!

At this point in my life, having lived through and witnessed a fair amount of disaster, I can honestly tell you that the most tangible moments of God's nearness have come in the darkest moments. We have all heard the trite sayings about hope in the toughest hours, we have all been admonished to hang in there another day, and we have all known of others who displayed heroic endurance in the face of overwhelming odds. To know God's keeping power personally is another thing entirely.

Through all the messes in my life I have come to know the grace of God and the severity of sin's destructive power. Looking back now, I remember when, in graduate school, I wrote out a top-ten list of things I wanted God to accomplish in my life. At the top of that list I placed the desire to know, deeply, the grace of God. What I have found in my life is that the riches of His grace are most apparent during hardship. God's nearness in the tough times has assured me that even when I cannot see it, He is there in the details.

Next on the list was the desire to know just how damning the reality of sin truly is. I have seen the curses of sin over the years, but I have fallen over and over again into the wondrous hands of grace. With Donne, I can attest that any and all battering is worth it. Whatever it takes to know God intimately, I'm still signing on. I still believe the church is the hope of the world. Katrina reminds me that neither politics, nor government, nor wealth, nor city leadership, nor any "humanitarian effort" can offer the healing needed in times like this. That kind of healing of the soul comes only from above.

As I look back, I think the greatest emotional, psychological, and spiritual struggle came from my questioning where God was and how He could possibly use for good the chaotic situations in which I found myself. I don't have all of the answers, and I won't answer all of the questions on this side of heaven, yet I have come to know that even in the waiting room of life, God is present and at work.

As I look back on that January day, the thirteenth, when my grandmother passed away, I now see that God was at work even then. On that apparently "unlucky" day, my grandmother's passing was more than a life expiring before my eyes. She had finally overcome her last storm and moved on to her reward, and she left me with the encouraging message that God was soon to give me a new start in life. That prediction has come to fruition.

In the last year, God has blessed me with the privilege of aiding in the start-up of a new church in New Orleans (another item on my top-ten list), He has fanned into flame a renewed desire for teaching and preaching. And He has given me the grace to write this work, which I pray is of some value to a few (yet another item on my top-ten list).

Historically, the number thirteen has been a good one for me. I am in no way a numerologist and not one to typically look for God in such things. However, when I was growing up playing baseball and church softball, I wore the number thirteen. I was married on Friday the thirteenth. And exactly one year before my grandmother's death (January 13, 2004) I was part of an investment transaction that has been the highlight of my career in the secular world.

The brokering of a deal for the placement of the famous 1913 Liberty Head Nickel (one of only five in the world) for $3 million was publicized as the "largest retail transaction for a single coin in the history of the rare coin market." For a coin guy, that's as good as it gets. It was a great deal of fun to be part of such a transaction, and it had been in the works for a long time. The story went around the globe via television, newspapers, radio, and the Internet. The greatest enjoyment in the whole thing, however, came from the fact that the investor for whom I secured the specimen was a godly man, and had come to be a good friend. My relationship with him, and the lessons I learned from the construction of the deal, would come to be a source of God's grace in my life. I knew, deep within, for some reason beyond its being a career highlight, that this event would be a benchmark date for me.

My grandmother strutted as proud as a peacock as she told anyone who would listen about the coin her grandson had sold. If anyone showed up at her house in the middle of the day, they were going to have to watch the videos, read the papers, and listen to the radio interviews about her now "famous" grandson and the nickel. Lucky 13! Hindsight often provides us the reminder that God has sent hints of His presence all along the way. If we were more able and willing to trust Him throughout the journey, we would regularly hear the whispers of His plan even in the midst of disaster. He does have a plan, and it's a plan for our good. No matter how much destruction we see around us, He is at work.

Jeremiah, often called the "weeping prophet," reminds us of this truth. This prophet of God, called to tell of God's dealing with humanity, experienced great pain in his ministry. Jeremiah's task, his calling, was to speak to a nation that was turning a deaf ear to God. Why God chooses some of His servants to experience great success and ease in this life while others He assigns the tougher road is not for us to know. The message that comes to all of us, however, is this: He has a plan. His plan, not to be measured by the luxuries around us or the numbers found in our pews, is a plan for His working all things for good and for His purposes. In His purposes and in His plan, we prosper. No matter how strong or how devastating the storm, we have a hope and a future. I have found this to be true. God's promise to us is recorded in the book of the weeping prophet, which bears his name: "'For I know the plans I have for you,' declares the LORD, 'plans for wholeness and not for evil, to give you a future and a hope'" (Jer. 29:11). That's the word for all of us who follow His plan for salvation, and that's the promise for any city or nation that will follow hard after Him.

"They Also Serve Who Only Stand and Wait": Lessons from John Milton

The tens of thousands of Hurricane Katrina victims held captive by the rising floodwaters waited for days to receive help. The dramatic helicopter rescues captured by the camera lens will remain etched in our minds forever. Stories of tragic events and criminal activity became more frequent as those awaiting rescue turned to their own devices for provision amidst the storm. Looting, violence, and gunfire aimed at police and rescue teams shocked everyone watching. Looking on, most of us thought, "How could they?"

In more recent days since the storm, we have seen stories of hope and goodness. New Orleans has been opened for business, and residents are making their way back to begin the process of rebuilding. For some, however, like those in the hardest hit areas of the ninth ward, rather than rebuilding, the return is still a a search and salvage operation for the few things that may not have been washed away forever. Residents continue to debate and ponder what the new "footprint" of the city will mean for their rebuilding and their future. Many of the displaced continue to look for and find small glimpses of hope.

One woman, Cheryl, returned to her home in St. Bernard Parish where the waters were over the roofs. Upon entering the mold-infested home and making her way to the bedroom, she happened upon a jewelry box, still intact, containing a ring that had been in the family many generations. She wept, thanking God for "small miracles" in the wake of so much loss. Back in her house for only a few hours, like many others, she will have to wait a long time before she can really return "home." This is the hard part. How does one wait, and wait, and wait, and still trust that a master plan is unfolding? How does one, dealing with the weight of enormous loss, wait with grace and poise? With so much seemingly senseless destruction all around, how does a person continue to hope?

John Milton (1608-1674) was and is an enormous figure in the world of literature. His seminal work *Paradise Lost* resides on a short list of the greatest poems ever written. Another of his works, *When I Consider How My Light Is Spent,* a short poem penned amidst his battle with blindness, is critical to understanding the life, thought, and substance of this epic writer. It relates to our discussion regarding the storms of our souls because in it Milton wrestles honestly before an all-powerful God who holds in His hands the ability to quell all storms and heal at any moment.

Oftentimes, amidst the hard realities of this life, we wonder, "Where is our help?" Like those caught by the waters of Katrina, stranded in a city that seems to be caving in moment by moment, we often stand mystified by the severity of our dilemma and the lack of apparent response from a helper. How do we understand this situation? How do we make any sense of what is happening?

The images of angry, starving, dehydrated citizens of the world's only remaining superpower, struggling for survival in a city crushed by the brutality of nature, humbled us, startled us, and left us wondering what to make of this tragedy. What do we do when life saps us of all our resources, ups the ante on our misery, and seemingly mocks us? How do we move on when the world changes so much for the worse from one day to the next? One day everything is light, and then the next day darkness falls and remains. So much changed, in just one day, for the inhabitants of the city of New Orleans. The Big Easy, in a matter of twenty-four hours, was turned into the nation's Big Dilemma. What now? What do we do with such a mess? What can we do while our lives are put back together? How do we wait on God during such an ongoing disaster?

John Milton dealt with these questions as he struggled with blindness. This brilliant mind, determined to know and understand what life was about, wrestled with a debilitating condition. From the beginning of his life, John Milton was a gifted learner. He mastered his studies and was adept at languages. He was a hungry scholar. Satisfying that hunger, of course, entailed a great deal of reading and writing. Reading and writing require sight. Early on, Milton felt the call of God to pen the greatest English poem ever put to paper. The result of that call, and the affirmation of that call in the minds of many, is *Paradise Lost*, which was his attempt to "justify the ways of God to men."

Milton's life was not an easy one. Scholars point to three major periods in his life, each characterized by difficulty and struggle. By 1663, all of it came to a crescendo. All of the wrestling with God amidst various and intense disasters led up to his greatest contribution to literature. The *Norton Anthology of English Literature* makes reference to this struggle: "In 1663, Milton married his third wife, Elizabeth Minshull, and in blindness, poverty, defeat, and relative isolation, he set about completing a poem justifying the ways of God to men."

While *Paradise Lost* is referred to as Milton's greatest achievement, an investigation of what it offers is not our aim here. Rather, a brief glimpse of one of his most intense struggles is our concern. For the justifications of God's actions explained in *Paradise Lost* stem from a life of wrestling with physical, emotional, financial, and spiritual disaster. *When I Consider How My Light Is Spent* offers us a heartfelt and soul-stirring look at what it means to find God amidst disaster, and it helps direct us to that place where we can say with Milton, at the end of the journey, "God's ways are higher than our ways, and He truly has us in His hands."

> When I consider how my light is spent,
> Ere half my days, in this dark world and wide,
> And that one talent which is death to hide,
> Lodged with me useless, though my soul more bent
> To serve therewith my Maker, and present
> My true account, lest he returning chide;
> "Doth God exact day-labor, light denied?"
> I fondly ask; but Patience to prevent
> That murmur, soon replies, "God doth not need"
> Either man's work or his own gifts; who best
> Bear His mild yoke, they serve Him best. His state
> Is kingly. Thousands at his bidding speed
> And post o'er land and ocean without rest:
> They also serve who only stand and wait.

What is Milton saying with this powerful poem? The lessons are extensive, but I would like to call our attention to a few of the most relevant messages. First and foremost, through his struggles Milton has his faulty view of his importance corrected. How many of us quickly fall into self-pity when difficulty sets in? How many of us, deceived by our own preoccupation with our "need," turn to bitterness and resentment when we don't get what we want as soon as we want it? And how is it that people we once thought were good look so bad when life gets challenging?

Looters are a case in point. Images of looters running throughout New Orleans at our lowest moment were stunning. Where did these people think they were going with stereos, radios, televisions, and Nike tennis shoes? No dry land on which to run in those shoes, no one to play basketball with, no electricity for radio or television or stereos, and no way to hide from the cameras. What were they thinking?

Milton, like Job, has his inflated view of his importance sharply corrected by the Creator of the universe. "God doth not need" us. We tend to get that thought backward: "We doth not need" God. His desire is that we might see our need of Him during desperate times. Desperation ought to send us upward. Once we understand, regardless of our "success" in this world, just how little we are in light of God's universe and plan, we can begin to look up to God in gratitude for our lives and humbly turn to Him when the odds are against us.

Milton writes also of his new awareness of the value in waiting. In contrast to the all-conquering Christian superman ideal, we see heroism of faith in this poem put on display by humbly and peacefully waiting and trusting a power other than ourselves to work out the plan. We do not like waiting. At all costs we avoid the long lines at the grocery, we buy express passes at the Disney theme parks, we TiVo, we eat "fast food," we microwave, and we pay through the nose for anything and everything to be shipped next day air. These things seem trivial at first glance, but in reality this frame of mind does, indeed, transfer to our view of how God should work in our lives. Our expectation is for God to hurry up and fix us and our situation. This greatest loss in such a view of

God is the resulting lack of peace and growth in the journey toward spiritual maturity. God values the journey, and He uses all its twists and turns to unfold His plan, His glorious plan, in our lives.

We see this truth again and again in scriptural accounts of heroes of faith, like Joseph, Abraham, Moses, Paul, and many more. In any inspiring historical account of a life well lived, and in every account of heroes of faith, we see a life filled with grace and triumph amidst overwhelming odds. We do not admire people who always have it easy. We admire those who exhibit courage, strength, and integrity — all of which are displayed in difficult situations. At some point, those who turn to God amidst this misery inflicted by Katrina (or any disaster) will find newness of life, depth of character, and increased poise and purpose.

Katrina, like all major disasters, has put many lives seemingly on hold. So many of us, during the weeks and months following the storm, felt as if everything were moving in slow motion. "What about our plans, God? What now? What about the deal I was working on? What about the house I was building? What about *me?*" This disaster, like all disasters, is out of place in our lives. This should not be. For New Orleans and the Gulf Coast region affected by the storm, it is as if the entire history of a vibrant region has been brought to an abrupt halt. What good can come from this?

Beyond what we have already investigated here, Milton's poem offers us some very practical insights into this subject. These truths give us some concrete foundational instruction upon which we can build our lives when we find ourselves in God's waiting room:

(1) It is worth the wait.

Anytime God does not give us what we want when we want it, we must remember that it is for our good. We cannot fathom what God has in store for us in the unfolding of His plans. If we can keep ourselves from attempting to direct His hand so often, we will find ourselves much more at peace. Any perceived delay is in reality God's perfect timing. Much greater is the joy for those who have worked and waited, prayed and hoped over the long haul. In

God's plan, a pleasure postponed is in reality a joy increased. How thrilled were the Red Sox to finally win the World Series again after "all those years?" How thrilled will the people of a rebuilt New Orleans be when the Saints finally win the Super Bowl? (Okay, maybe some things are never meant to happen, but you get the point.) The scriptures tell us, "No eye has seen, no ear has heard, no mind has conceived, what God has prepared for those who love him" (1. Cor. 2:9 NIV). It's worth the wait.

(2) There is strength in the wait.

Typically, men and women of great inner strength developed that gusto through a great deal of time and hardship. There are no shortcuts to greatness. Great strength is the exception, because so few are willing to wait for their time. It is too tempting to settle for mediocrity, which comes so much quicker and so much easier. How does a world-class athlete get to the place where the body performs so perfectly that it looks effortless?

Years of conditioning, training, and pain are the requirement for that kind of accomplishment. When a man or woman of God endures what seems like endless suffering, and in the face of that suffering exhibits marvelous grace, it is a thing of beauty. That kind of strength comes from a heart dedicated to waiting on God. The strength to wait on Him settles in when we let go of our craving for ease and comfort. That is a hard thing for Americans. Who has not been astounded by stories like those of Joni Erickson Tada and Corrie ten Boom? These women demonstrated godly strength in the face of terrifying difficulty. As we surrender ourselves, our hopes, ambitions, understanding of life, and all that we are to God, we find hope even in places of hardship, and we find a supernatural strength welling up within us. We can make it through.

(3) There is character in the wait.

Have you seen the movie *Mr. Holland's Opus*? In that film Mr. Holland became a high school music teacher by default, but he ultimately came to find his life's purpose in instilling vision, passion, and a love of learning in the kids he taught. At the end of the movie Mr. Holland is let go from his job of many years, and he is heartbroken. He is tempted to question whether his career meant anything at all. This man, who early in life aspired to be a great composer, is now at the end of his journey as a teacher and is feeling totally dispensable. As he is gathering his things from his office and leaving the school campus for the last time, he hears noise coming from the auditorium.

With his wife tagging along, he ventures into the auditorium to see what is going on. What he walks into is a testament to the power of character, his character. The auditorium is full of students, current and those from years gone by. They are all there to celebrate a life lived with character. Though Mr. Holland never made it as a composer, he made a difference in the lives of countless youth. His true opus, they tell him, is the lives he transformed. I have watched it twenty times and never once with a dry face.

As we go through this life, we must remember that our character is what is most important. "For what shall it profit a man, if he shall gain the whole world, and lose his own soul?" (Matt. 16:26 KJV). If we abandon character for selfish ambition, we miss the boat. Any legacy we leave will stand or fall based upon our character. It is not about the size of our house or bank account, and it is not about the toys in our garage. All of that, as we have seen, can go ten feet under in a matter of hours. When all our things are lost, and we get "displaced," what is inside still remains. When all we have left is what we see in the mirror, reality hits home. Character of soul is what matters. The character and integrity of the structure of our soul is what will determine how we weather the storm.

(4) There is grace in the wait.

Milton, who gradually "watched" his sight diminish and eventually totally leave him, wrestled intensely with God's purpose in this illness. At the end of the struggle, God gave him a remarkable glimpse of His grace. God birthed in Milton an amazing poem that crystallizes the heavenly perspective on disaster. Milton came to understand that we do not need to have it all "put together" to be used by God. He came to see that we have value before the Creator just for showing up. God's ability to love us and to use us is not hindered by our disability. As we wait on God, hungering and thirsting to know what amazing accomplishments lie ahead for us, what really matters is just that—waiting on God.

This waiting, godly waiting, amounts to no more than a joyful, restful, strong, grace-filled acceptance that God's agenda for us is enough. It is up to Him to show the extravagance of His grace in our lives. As we cooperate with that purpose, waiting on Him is life, and that abundantly (John 10:10). In the rubble of disaster, the message is clear: The clock has not run out on us. God is not finished. The best may be ahead. Remember, John Milton wrote *Paradise Lost* while he was blind! God is the "treasure hidden in a field" (Matt. 13:44 NIV), the "pearl of great price" (Matt. 13:46 KJV), "the beginning and the end" (Rev. 21:6 KJV), our "all in all" (1 Cor. 15:28 NIV)—and He is worth waiting on!

(5) Waiting reveals truth, absolute truth.

We live in a culture overcome with opinion. Just listen to all of the opinions on how the city of New Orleans ought to be rebuilt. There are fights over when to allow residents to reenter the city, what to do about FEMA contracts, which areas of the city to bull-doze and which to rebuild, who is to blame for the havoc, who gets press time and who does not, and who will pay for all of this mess. Beyond opinions on this disaster, Americans embrace the idea that truth is relative and each opinion is as valuable as the next. The contemporary American view is that all beliefs are equal. Essentially, as a culture, we are making the ridiculous assumption that no absolute truth exists. This is, of course, stated by our talk-show host-philosophers, absolutely.

What God shows us, however, in the waiting room of disaster, is that we all crave one sure answer for our pain and loss. At the juncture between dreams and nightmares, we cry out for truth. We all want the dream life, we all want protection from the nightmare.

We all give ourselves credit for the good, and we are too tempted to blame Mother Nature for the bad. In moments of misery, varying opinions just do not carry the same weight as firm truth. Truth is what we all need when all is lost. Mothers who are losing a child to a terminal illness want someone to make sense of things for them. Adult children who have lost an elderly parent as a result of someone's failure to evacuate a nursing home want answers. Pain, loss, and waiting thrust us in the direction of God.

Just as we sit with family and friends in hospital waiting rooms while our loved ones undergo life-threatening surgical procedures, so we also wait with a hunger for hope of good news from above when all our hopes are fading away. One friend, whose business and life were dramatically affected by the hurricane, recently told me, "I am just looking for some hope." Disasters propel us to find the source of hope and truth. The truth is that there is hope. That hope is found only in the Truth. Jesus said, "I am the way, the truth, and the life" (John 14:6 KJV). He is absolutely our only hope.

I have come to see the reality of these practical truths throughout my life as I have wrestled with God during my own personal disasters. So many times I have thought, "This is another roadblock, another step backward." In reality, as I look back now, I see that God was and is at work. God was and is at work in the lives of all of those impacted by Hurricane Katrina. Our view of God, as was the case for Milton, is being reworked as we deal with darkness.

Our prayer must be that God will give us spiritual eyes to see what He is saying to us. In our own spiritual blindness, we seem to be missing the point. Just as Milton could not understand how God's plan for this great scholar, writer, and poet could possibly unfold amidst blindness, so we too lack eyes to see what God is up to in this present disaster. Could it be that God has placed us in the waiting room of life in order that we might think more seriously — as a city, a people, a nation — about who God is and how far we are falling short of His call to us?

All the rebuilding timelines and projections point to this being a very long wait. It will take years of extremely hard work to get the city of New Orleans and the Gulf Coast region moving again. For our own good and the good of our county, we ought to use this time in waiting to reflect upon where we have been and where we are going. Now, just months following the devastation of Katrina, we are hearing about the possibility of the coming bird flu pandemic. What if another huge storm lies ahead for a nation without eyes to see and ears to hear the voice of God?

As bad as the devastation of Katrina has been, all the experts are now telling us it could have been much worse. If God does not have our undivided attention now, what will it take? God's ways, as Milton found out, are indeed justifiable. Like Job and Milton, we often view ourselves higher than we ought to. We are not the end of all things. When we find ourselves at the mercy of "nature," this reality comes painfully close to home.

Standing amidst such catastrophe, we have no power as humans to "speak" our desires into existence as some preachers or "positive thinkers" might suggest. What was true for John Milton is true for us: No man-centered theology will fix this mess. God alone can make sense of this situation. The answers are there if we are willing to listen.

In moments like these we must simply recognize that His ways are higher than our ways, humbly throw ourselves before Him, and trust in His grace. Only a word spoken from God can heal this kind of hurt. Though our present experience may confuse us, we must trust God's desire and ability to always be working for our good. As Alister McGrath has written in his book, *The Mystery of the Cross*, "The theology of the Cross draws our attention to the sheer unreliability of experience as a guide to the presence and activity of God. God is active and present in his world, quite independently of whether we experience him as being so. Experience declared that God was absent from Calvary, only to have its verdict humiliatingly overturned on the third day." As McGrath explains, whether or not we experience God in a neatly packaged box we have conjured up in our own heads does not determine the reality of His workings on this planet and in our lives.

PART TWO

DISASTER RECOVERY— REBUILDING THE SOUL

Hear, you deaf, and look, you blind, that you may see!
Who is blind but my servant,
or deaf as my messenger whom I send?
Who is blind as my dedicated one,
or blind as the servant of the LORD?
He sees many things, but does not observe them;
his ears are open, but he does not hear.
The LORD was pleased, for his righteousness' sake,
to magnify his law and make it glorious.
But this is a people plundered and looted;
they are all of them trapped in holes and hidden in prisons;
they have become plunder with none to rescue,
spoil with none to say, "Restore!"
Who among you will give ear to this,
will attend and listen for the time to come?
Who gave up Jacob to the looter,
and Israel to the plunderers?
Was it not the LORD, against whom we have sinned,
in whose ways they would not walk,
and whose law they would not obey?
So he poured on him the heat of his anger
and the might of battle;
it set him on fire all around, but he did not understand;
it burned him up, but he did not take it to heart.
(Isa. 42:18-25)

What Do We Make of This Mess?

Earlier, I suggested that if we are to make progress in dealing with the disasters in our lives we must start by gaining a proper perspective on life as a whole. That is to say, if we are to find any credible answers to our dilemma, we must ask the right questions. This idea of right questions preceding meaningful answers is not only the subject of much philosophical inquiry, it is supported in scripture.

In this passage from Isaiah, we find a very interesting scenario unfolding as we read. The spokesman of God does not, at this moment, comfort his hearers with delightful pronouncements of blessing, abundance, success, and good fortune. Rather, the word of God to the listener is one of questioning — intense, direct, and corrective questioning. We will find comfort, covering, hope, and a future as we continue with God's word to His people, but we must begin by evaluating what this message of discipline is intended to address.

Where is God in the midst of this "natural" disaster? This is an important question, and the answer may be more unsettling than we are willing to admit. In order to gain some perspective on God's presence in this disaster and what He may be saying, doing, and accomplishing, we must rewind the tape a bit.

September 11, 2001, was a very dark day in our national history. I recall vividly where I was, who I was with, and how people around me responded to the events as they unfolded. I was making my daily forty-mile commute from the suburbs of New Orleans into the downtown central business district. Just as I was nearing the end of the causeway bridge, NPR broke in with a sudden announcement, "A plane has crashed into one of the towers of the World Trade Center in New York City."

At that moment, the media suspected what most listeners suspected: Something had gone wrong with a routine commercial airliner, and a sad event had just transpired. My initial thoughts were that in the days ahead we would hear of an engine failure, the search for the black box, and other typical crash information. Reality set in not too many minutes later, when as I was making my way into the skyscraper where I work, I heard everyone talking about the tragic event and the unfolding drama.

As I got off the elevator and walked through the doors of my office, everyone had gathered in a room where we typically have our morning meetings. On this day, no such meeting was to take place. Our technology staff had quickly gotten a television signal up and running in the meeting room, and our company gathered to see what was happening. Just as many of us were arriving, we witnessed the second plane make its ill-fated and unthinkable descent into the second tower. That moment, for all of us, was a defining one, one that changed all of our lives. Or was it?

As we, and others all across the country, realized the magnitude of the event unfolding before our eyes, pain, horror, shock, numbness, and fear set in. I looked around that room that day and watched carefully and thoughtfully as many of my peers wept. Just like those in the towers that day, we were a company populated, largely, with well-to-do brokers and employees. With all the security of substantial incomes, frequent travel, big houses, and all the benefits that the "American Dream" offered, few of us were really considering the ultimate issues in life. That changed in an instant on 9-11. On that day, Americans became a more thoughtful, spiritually minded, and sober people.

Even away from New York City, as Americans, we found it hard to focus, work, or play. The tales of those who lived in the Big Apple at the time of the disaster spoke of the world's most vibrant city coming to a sudden standstill. Entertainment, ball games, dining — it all came to a screeching halt. What seemed so crucial to our lives beforehand just lost its brilliance amidst the darkness of that day. News stories around the country told of Americans' renewed concern over spiritual matters and ultimate issues. Pulpits across the country suggested that our attentions, amidst the pain, would be turned back to God, and an American revival of the soul would make us better, stronger, more God-centered.

Shortly after the tragic befalling of our national monuments, monuments to our superiority economically, democratically, and militarily, I led a prayer service in our office building. The president of the United States had just called for a national day of prayer, and I was asked to lead a service for people in our office. As the preparations were being made, the event extended beyond our office and eventually became an event for our entire building. Some two hundred people showed up for that service.

During the service, several others and I read prayers we had prepared or shared thoughts. We showed slides with images, stills of the unfolding of the disaster. The images were vivid and still remain in my heart and soul to this day. There were images of a city in ruins and people falling or jumping from windows, having seconds earlier made a decision on the better, most expedient way to die in that moment of terror. We left that service in silence. We left with a prayer in our hearts for God to turn the very core of our beings toward Him in the midst of such unfathomable tragedy. And I honestly think many left that service with a prayer to God that He would cause them to live a different, better life.

In 9-11, we saw just how desperate life on this planet can become amidst seemingly mindless evil. But it was not our first glimpse of that reality, and it surely won't prove to be our last. The American psyche dealt with this kind of thing at Pearl Harbor and, more recently, at Columbine and Oklahoma City. Each time we are dealt a blow of this magnitude, we see and hear reports, studies, and pronouncements that America will grieve, but she will come back more thoughtful, spiritual, and resilient. And each time, we all hope that is indeed the case. But is it?

Is it true that after the initial pain, shock, horror, grieving, and processing of these events we come back better people? And if not, how do we accomplish this change in attitude and action? If we fail to become a more God-minded people, are there consequences? Does God intend to speak to us amidst these national disasters and the disasters of our individual lives? If so, what is He trying to say? Is God, in keeping with His loving character as a good heavenly Father, determined to teach His children to follow hard after Him even if it requires an increased form of discipline for those hard of hearing? These questions, I believe, are critical for our future as a country. These questions, and the answers to them, determine where we will end up and what our future will be like.

I maintain the position that I am not one of the dreaded, much-maligned, and "stereotypical" doomsday pulpit shouters. Parenthetically, however, I must point out that in scripture we do find God sending spokespersons to be trumpeters of divine wrath. A word of clarification as to what I am suggesting and what I am not suggesting should be given here.

What I am suggesting is the possibility that many events in our nation's recent past, and most recently Hurricane Katrina, are intended by God to wake us up from our habitual neglect of pursuing life lived under the direct gaze of a holy, loving, and life-sustaining Creator. What I am not suggesting is that I know for sure, or that God has told me directly, that Hurricane Katrina was sent directly by Him, at this precise moment in time, for the specific cause of bringing judgment upon America for its lack of holiness and all of its offenses against Him.

America is indeed lacking in its degree of passion for a holy national life, and as Americans we certainly are guilty of many breaches of God's directives. The depths of our transgressions as a nation are readily apparent, and should not be taken lightly. The reality is that God is always calling us to a more committed life, and when His message is not getting through, He turns up the volume. The reality, I fear, despite the numerous opportunities for America to hear God's call to a better way, is that we are not hearing what God is saying to us, we are not seeing with spiritual eyes what God is attempting to show us.

In the days since 9-11, we have drifted back to our idolatrous ways. *Desperate Housewives* is our favorite television program, racial tensions continue to mount, our thirst remains for pleasure, and our devoted rage against any form of absolute truth goes unabated. We aspire to promote the tolerance of all things without any regard for the destruction that certain tolerances bring to families and souls. The murdering of the unborn and the abandonment of any credible definition of family leaves us a nation on the verge of ever-increasing societal disaster. Might God be speaking to us about such issues in these days through the events we see unfolding before us, personally and as a country?

May we have ears to hear the Spirit of God upon the winds coming our way. At a minimum, in this disaster and any disaster we may face personally, is it not true that God wishes to teach us something about ourselves? Pain, suffering, and loss always bring us to a place of reevaluation, questioning, and consideration of ultimate reality. Has God intended it so? Let's get back to Isaiah.

Listen Up!

In the above passage from Isaiah, we find a God who has immense love for His chosen people. The nation of Israel, as history and scripture proclaim, was, in God's plan for the world, the people through whom God chose to establish His plan for all of humanity. History is replete with the dialogue, controversy, and horror stemming from this proposition. In order to avoid going into a book-length exposition of Israel's place in the divine plan and in history, we must assume here, for the sake of argument, that this nation does indeed fit into God's redemptive plan as a crucial hinge-point. Assuming then that Israel is under the blessing and obligation of this reality, it is important to know what God expects of His people with regard to the way they follow the plan.

The passage from Isaiah quoted above clearly reveals that somewhere along the road God's chosen nation independently decided to take a detour. This nation, promised great blessing by a loving God, made the conscious decision to create a new map, one in direct conflict with the one given to them by their Leader. Apparently, like the huge neon orange-and-white-striped signs we see at major road-repair construction sites, God had sent warning after warning. At every turning point, God had placed caution signs that were repeatedly ignored by His people. God's call to His people was not being heard. His warnings were not registering with a people more concerned with the trappings around them.

His people had grown confident in their own plans, desires, pursuits, and ideologies. God decided it was time to send a call loud and clear. By God's design, the emergency horn would sound louder and louder until heard. God's love, in discipline, would make an attempt to get His children back on the road to recovery. But, you might ask, "Is that truly loving?"

It would seem to make sense, just as any financial counselor who truly has a client's interests in mind would lay out a clear game plan for success. So too would a caring parent who wants the best for a child lay out a plan for healthy growth and development. Any good doctor, aware of an individual's reckless behavior, would go to great lengths to warn his patient of the risk involved in chemical abuse of any kind. Likewise, a good judge, probation officer, or counselor would warn a paroled defendant of the future peril should he go back to a former way of life. Common sense would inform us that if indeed God loved His people, He would want to present to them a plan for life that could be followed and that offered them the opportunity for blessing. Further, any good financial planner, coach, employer, or parent would want to point out the pitfalls along the way to prevent major disaster.

We see just how committed we are to this idea in the stories we read about Enron, WorldCom, and so many other businesses involved in scams. No one would think it sensible or morally defensible for a person in leadership to intentionally lead astray those under his care. Why would we then expect anything less of God? Unloving parents are those who abandon their children, leaving them without means for provision, care, love, and direction. Worse are those parents who would intentionally mislead their children, knowing full well that destruction would be the result for following the path set before them.

Moreover, any good parent or leader would provide a means to follow the plan, reinforce the plan with the promise of blessings that derive from following it, and provide warnings and discipline for deviation from it. The warnings and discipline, of course, are intended to bring the hearers to their senses and get them back on track. Could God be speaking to America? Does He use natural disasters to reveal a sickness of soul to those He cares about? Is there something we are missing? Why do we fail to hear God's voice of warning and see His hand at work?

The problem in which we find ourselves as citizens of the world's one remaining superpower is that we no longer want to embrace a common-sense view, let alone a spiritual-sense view, of morality — unless of course, it fits into our own pursuit of pleasure and comfort. Our view of spirituality, even within some churches, has grown so decidedly contrary to God's plan that He has no choice but to raise the volume on His call to us. God's own "church" in America has come to resemble so closely the culture at large that in many settings the church is not discernable from the culture in which it operates. That culture, given a rich heritage of blessing and providence by God, has for some time been turning a deaf ear to the warnings of God.

Just as God warned Israel of the folly in turning away from Him to worship false gods, so He may be warning us in America of the same danger today. He may be trying to tell us that we have turned away from Him to the idols of sensuality, the false security of riches, the addiction to pleasure, and the astonishing craving for the renouncement of absolute truth. As Americans, we want desperately, against all common sense, to suggest that all truths are equal even when they contradict one another. This kind of moral, intellectual, and spiritual suicide, like the doctrine of assisted suicide, is beginning to show its consequences. The outcome of such thinking is a society in moral and civil decay before our very eyes. "In God we trust," a now-debated doctrine in our halls of justice, is on the verge of becoming extinct.

We cry out for God's help amidst disaster, yet we have systematically removed Him from our schools and public forums. The "right" of women to choose has trumped the doing of "right." We should be aware that the worship of the "right to choose" will reap, perhaps, a morbid consequence down the line when those who choose the termination of the unborn early in life are eventually called upon to choose whether or not to care for the elderly when they are frail or economic and emotional burdens. A trampling of the sanctity of life may now very well end in the trampling of an entire generation of people. When created beings hold their "right" to be supreme, all sensible moral restraint is at risk. The whim of individuals to choose and the retreat from absolute truth are both part of a war raged against reason.

The struggle to live rightly has been replaced by a battle against the "right" side of the political spectrum.

When is it ever right to choose wrong, I must ask? What happens if the desire for choosing contradicts all rational and moral judgment? What if rational and moral judgment itself is defined a thousand or a million different ways? Who is right when no one wants to say that right exists? The proliferation of the "truth" that no absolute truth exists is, literally, nonsense. One cannot absolutely pronounce that no absolute truth exists. The very suggestion is contradictory and without logical basis. Yet, here we are in America, a "Christian" nation, and we find, even in the finest of our academic institutions, this wholehearted embrace of intellectual, moral, and spiritual bankruptcy.

This kind of "free" thinking is the very curriculum for our developing leaders, and has been for far too long. Is it any wonder we see, in moments of great pain and desolation, looters abandoning all moral restraint, while their city lies in waste? Rather than looking for a way to help those drowning in the rising waters, Americans were taking all they could get at an opportune moment. But it was their choice, was it not? Who is to say whether it was right or wrong? Who draws the lines? Where are the boundaries?

That brings us back to Isaiah. The message from this spokesman of God was simple and direct. According to God, His people had moved beyond the boundaries of His kingdom. In doing so, God's people had opened themselves up to a world of difficulty and decay. This decay showed up in the nation of Israel in the form of war, murder, adultery, idolatry, sexual immorality, harlotry, homosexuality, neglect of the poor, and spiritual distortion. These, among other less-than-desirable qualities, came to define those who had been chosen by God to live lives of blessing, goodness, and peace. Could it be that God in His love for us as a people, a city, and a nation has allowed, sent, or intended to use this most recent disaster to call us — a people similar in too many ways to the nation of Israel represented in this passage from Isaiah — to a life more in line with His calling for us?

Not only is it possible, but it is exactly how He has worked throughout biblical history. When people He is calling to Himself act in ways not in keeping with family life in His kingdom, the Father extends His loving hand of discipline to bring them back in line and protect them from greater danger (Prov. 13:24). God knows what life beyond the boundaries is like. The farther from home we get, the worse life becomes. At times the Father will increase the pressure, and sharpen the discipline, to get our attention. When His children turn a deaf ear to His wisdom, He finds a way to be heard.

Rather than this action being a sign of His narrow-minded and prudish inclination, it is a sign of His marvelous love and hunger for our good. Just as He assured the nation of Israel that they were the "apple of his eye" (Deut. 32:10), so he assures us, as His people today, that He is for us and not against us (Rom. 8:31). He uses all things, we are told in His Word, to work out His good plan for us (Rom. 8:28). All things — even disaster! He will mold, use, send, allow, and make all things turn out for the good of His children.

Life beyond the boundary, as the Prodigal Son found out (Luke 15:11ff), is no life worth pursuing. The quest for pleasure at every hand, as Solomon discovered, is not enough to quench the soul. The thirst for sexuality outside of the plan of God ends in confusion, disease, psychological disarray, and broken families. In His plan, as is revealed in scripture, our sexuality finds its most exhilarating and soul-inspiring fulfillment. Life on the other side of the fence, God knows, only provides different grass. Inside the boundaries of God's playground, abundant life unfolds bigger and better than any fantasy displayed on the grandest of silver screens. Inside the boundaries of God are found the boundless heights of love, joy, peace, and life everlasting! America must come back to God's playground.

Life Beyond the Boundaries

It has been suggested that as a human race, a fallen race, we are never satisfied with the good God offers us. Had God allowed us one hundred wives, it has been suggested, we would have taken one hundred and one. Boundary breaking is in our nature, and scripture does indeed attest to this very fact. The first record of boundary breaking is found at the very beginning of the human story. In the garden, Adam and Eve were given so much, nearly everything. God, in His love, placed only one limit upon this couple, the crown of His creation. Creating them with the will to choose a life lived in devotion to Him, God offered them the world as their playground and merely asked that they keep a good distance from that which would bring the downfall of unhampered communion with Him. The boundary line had been drawn around the tree of the knowledge of good and evil. God went so far as to tell them why He drew this line in the sand, "For in the day that you eat of it, you shall surely die" (Gen. 2:17). It is interesting that the first boundary ever drawn is the very same boundary we are so bent on crossing today.

Our quest as human creations to define reality, good and evil, according to our opinions, remains the cause of our downfall today. In the academic institutions of our country, once intended to lead students to certainty and truth, we now find a bias against any suggestion that truth really exists. We are determined, as it has been suggested, to educate ourselves into imbecility. In our courts, we find the honoring of clever tactic, loophole navigation, and juror manipulation trumping justice, truth, and reality. On our televisions and silver screens, we see the fantastic portrayal of a false life that offers promises never fulfilled in the real world. Try living according to the philosophy of *Desperate Housewives,* and see just how wholesome, satisfying, and fulfilling your life becomes.

The Prodigal Son always discovers, sooner or later, that the life he always wanted is never found amidst the mud and mire of the pig's playground. As Americans, we have been blinded by fantasy, and lured away by the false promise of unending pleasure. Every drug addict knows that the thirst for pleasure always ends in hellish misery. Those hooked by the bait of pornography tell us of the shame and sleepless nights, the inability to see people beyond the physical. Success addicts tell us of the emptiness at the top after living a life devoted to crushing others for the sake of personal gain. We have been duped. Blake's words ring just as true today as the day they were penned:

> This life's dim Windows of the Soul
> Distorts the Heavens from Pole to Pole
> And leads you to believe a Lie
> When you see with, not thro', the Eye.

Malcolm Muggeridge, in his important work, *Jesus: The Man Who Lives,* calls our attention to this reality in a profound passage. Commenting on Blake's words, he writes:

> Thus Blake distinguishes between the fantasy that is seen with the eye and the truth that is seen through it. They are two clearly demarcated kingdoms; and passing from one to the other, from the kingdom of fantasy to the kingdom of reality, gives inexpressible delight.

It is indeed true that when we at last have the blinders removed and we are able to see the world from a divine viewpoint all things become new and our spirit soars. There is no greater moment in life than the one in which the soul finds focus and the exhilaration of newfound perspective comes rushing in.

Muggeridge again notes:

> In this kingdom of reality, Simone Weil tells us, nothing is so
> continually fresh and surprising, so full of sweet and perpetu-
> al ecstasy, as goodness; no desert so dreary, monotonous and
> boring as evil. . . . With how unutterable a longing does one
> yearn to leave the sunless land of fantasy and live for ever in
> the sunshine of reality!"

And so, until as individuals, communities, and a country, we
come to the place where we value God's wisdom and truth, we
cannot hope to find stability, insight, and growth amidst the disasters that come our way. If we are to begin to move on toward a
rebuilding effort that will be profitable for our future, we must
first see, with spiritual eyes, what God would have us to see about
ourselves in the dark moments of the soul. For when all around us
is darkness and debris, the eyes of the soul attuned to God still
have sight.

He is the God of wind and water (Mark 4:41), and He does have
plans for us (Jer. 29:11), even as the waters rise and the winds
blow. We must be able and willing to look and listen in order that
we might be built up better than we were before. No rebuilding
project, however well planned, funded, and implemented, can
hold up against the winds and waves sent from the hand of God.
Until He gets our attention, and submission, the winds will continue to blow upon our frame. His intentions for us are for our good.
His plan must be embraced. The choice, as they say, is ours. We
must choose wisely. Like all choices, consequences follow. God is
speaking. Are we listening? The Builder of builders offers us the
blueprint to life. Will we take Him up on His offer?

A Bigger Storm

There is currently a media storm brewing about the real potential of a global Avian flu pandemic. All major national and international bodies are investigating, preparing, and warning of the

implications of this threat. Economically, the global situation is charting new waters. For the first time in two decades, tangible assets, particularly precious metals, are surfacing as a major source for investment allocation. This is critically important because, as economists and financial counselors are aware, gold and other precious metals represent the asset of choice during times of economic upheaval, geo-political uncertainty, and international turmoil.

Moreover, gold's value rises as the strength of the U.S. dollar declines. Gold, historically, is the safe haven amidst times of economic disaster. Its fundamental function is crisis-oriented. The fact that economists and financial theorists are considering the reemergence of gold at this time points to the potential of a future much different from anything we have seen since the Great Depression. The forecasters are now predicting gold to climb to heights not seen in more than twenty-five years. In his article, "Attention Miners, the Canary Is Dead," Peter D. Schiff of Euro Pacific Capital recently commented: "A sharp increase in the price of gold is a warning signal that all is not well. It is a precursor to rising inflation, higher interest rates, reduced profits, and a general loss of confidence in financial assets." Simply put, when gold is doing well, all else may not be in as good a shape regardless of how we perceive it.

In the minds of many investors, this warning signal is never acknowledged. Economically speaking, this can lead to a major catastrophe. When we know all is not well we must make adjustments. To ignore the coming storm is to invite disaster. Unfortunately, many investors, at this critical moment in our financial history, are ignoring the signals and the underlying reality of the situation. Schiff writes, "It's as if a group of coal miners is casually standing around the body of a dead canary, confident that the bird met its demise due to natural causes."

The current preoccupation with gold specifically, and safe-haven investments generally, points to a big storm on the horizon. Mr. Schiff's words have some striking parallels to the state of our country, spiritually speaking. It is as if we are standing around, like the coal miners in Mr. Schiff's analogy, casually and with a total lack of recognition that our moral choices in America have everything to do with the ongoing death and decay of our society.

Poverty, class struggle, drug addiction, sexually transmitted disease, violence, broken homes, illiteracy, crime, racism, and many other ills prevalent in our culture do have a cause. It would appear, however, that we do not see the cause-and-effect link between our decisions and the strength of our nation. This over-sight, neglect, or intentional disregard for reality could very well lead to a storm beyond any we have seen to date.

With great concern for the potential of a major terrorist strike on our soil again, economic concerns globally, and geo-political turmoil running wild in Iran, Iraq, North Korea, and elsewhere, it may be time for us to give greater consideration to who we are and where we are headed. With America's oil resources in question and the threat of countries in the Middle East doing more to stress our reliance upon foreign sources of fuel, it is entirely possible, if not likely, that the cost of goods could rise sharply, and for some time to come. Huge trade deficits abound, borrowing is at historic levels, credit-card debt is off the charts, and the canary lies in front of us gasping for breath.

Was the Great Depression an anomaly? Is there no chance that America could see a storm of that magnitude again? Could the next major storm even eclipse any we have seen in our history? Should such a catastrophe come our way, will we have a safe haven? Can we hope to find protection from the storms ahead? If so, how?

"We Dodged a Bullet"

As bad as the scenes in New Orleans have been, we have been told that in actuality, "We dodged a bullet." Though the storm veered closer to us in the last hours of its approach, had it moved another fifty miles west, the devastation could have been unimaginably worse. Experts state that New Orleans was spared from total destruction because the city was not on the northeastern side of the storm. The suggestion that it could have been much worse is hard to comprehend for those of us who have seen the extent of the damage.

As we drive through the streets of the Greater New Orleans area, the scenes we witness are surreal. It is like something out of a science-fiction movie—cars on top of homes, boats in trees, gray ooze everywhere, homes reduced to piles of rubble, other homes moved from their foundations and relocated blocks away, and a smell that is hard to describe. It is eerie. The outcome of what has taken place has been life-altering for everyone caught in the wake of this brutally savage hurricane. Day after day, stories continue to be told about how Katrina has changed everything for so many.

John Gumm, a meteorologist in the New Orleans area, saw his life change in significant ways. His story was told by David Walker, a TV columnist from the New Orleans area. In the days following the storm, John and his family made the decision to pack up and relocate. With his wife, literally, on the verge of giving birth as the storm approached, John had become convinced that the nightmare scenario that had been feared for years was coming to pass. The last person John spoke to before leaving town was Mayor Ray Nagin. John Gumm's words to Mayor Nagin were, "This is the one we have feared." Soon thereafter, the mayor ordered a mandatory evacuation. After speaking with the mayor, Gumm left for the hospital to be with his wife as she was giving birth.

From there he was headed home to get ready for an immediate evacuation, knowing that the "big one" was on the way. He made contact with the news station and found out that the eye wall of the hurricane would be bearing down directly over his community in Slidell, Louisiana. There was no choice but to leave, and quick. There was a problem, however. John had just received a call from the hospital indicating that a potentially fatal situation had developed with his newborn. The two-mile trip back to the hospital took two hours. As he spoke to his wife on the way back to the hospital,

John was told that his new son might have Group B Strep, a potentially deadly illness. John had to make a decision. Knowing that Katrina would be bearing down on the family soon, and as a meteorologist, knowing just how deadly a situation that was, he decided to have the doctors give his son a hefty dose of antibiotics before he and his family headed out of town.

With no sleep over a forty-hour period and gridlock on the way to Nashville, John was wearing down. Stress from the work hours, fear of what the storm would bring, concern over the baby's health, and a car filled with family, animals, and a few belongings, was setting in. John and the family met up with relatives in Mississippi, where he changed his first diaper in the back of an SUV. From there, they went to Alabama, where they were able to witness on television the damage Katrina was doing to the city they had left behind. Eventually, John got the family to Nashville, went to a hospital where the report on the baby was good, and got his wife and son settled in with other members of the family. Upon returning to New Orleans and seeing the devastation of the city and of his own home, and recognizing the trauma his wife was undergoing, John decided it was time to make a change.

As a meteorologist, John's greatest dream had been to aid in helping the city plan for a massive Category-Five hurricane, and to get people out of harm's way. With that goal behind him, and his life entirely rearranged by the huge storm, John and his family, like so many others, packed up and moved on to other things. Now his sentiment is in keeping with that of so many others: "Katrina changed everything for us."

Katrina did indeed change so much for those caught in its crosshairs. Children were relocated. Many are still in new schools and having to make new friendships in distant cities. Adults are out of work. Moms and dads, in many cases, have to live apart from each other and their kids in order to survive. Businesses have left New Orleans, perhaps some 45 percent of total businesses were gone at one point. Thousands of people were living in shelters or hotels for months on end. Families are housing more people in limited space than they ever imagined possible. Cities across America are dealing with the realities of displaced, impoverished, and unemployed additions to their areas. And the city of New Orleans is dealing with conditions that it could never have imagined. Looting, violence, anger, stress, hopelessness, and political positioning have each had a hand in the aftermath of this storm. Life "as normal" is a thing of the past for hundreds of thousands of people. It is a mess, and the rebuilding will take years.

And yet, the experts suggest, "We dodged a bullet." What would life be like in a worst-case scenario in the city of New Orleans? What would ultimate catastrophe be like in our nation? What is to protect us from it? Do we have any assurance that the worst is behind us when we have seen so much disaster? Could it really be worse? Is this, as some are suggesting, an open door for the people of New Orleans to build bigger and better than before? Is it a historic growth opportunity?

I believe the answers to these questions depend greatly upon our response and our strategy. Further, I am inclined to believe that America, like New Orleans, has been sent a number of storms that are intended to force serious thought about the way we are building our nation at this moment in time. Is it possible that New Orleans received this blow as another gracious attempt by God to gain our attention? Is it possible that New Orleans was spared a worst-case scenario by God's compassionate hand? Is it at all possible that America, to this point, has been warned by God's discipline, yet spared total devastation because of the longsuffering nature and patience of God? In God's love and mercy, has He put off justice in order that we might have another chance to turn back to Him? And finally, we must ask, is there hope in turning back to Him? Is there a better way? Can we really rebuild our cities, our nation, and our souls?

The Gold Standard: Allocating for Disaster

It is more than interesting that New Orleans is center stage in this present story of disaster in America. The Big Easy, in micro-cosm, is a picture of the American soul at large. New Orleans, one of the top tourist destinations in the country year after year, embodies the American psyche in many ways. This city shows off many of our ideals on several levels. The quest for pleasure, fine dining, abandonment of moral restraint, entertainment around every turn, sexual freedom, political corruption, poverty, racism, educational and economic deprivation, and many other societal ills are contained in this city on the river. That is not to say that New Orleans does not have many wonderful characteristics. The point is that New Orleans' bad side offers us a valuable peek at our national moral dilemma. The dark side of New Orleans and our nation must be addressed if we are to rebuild and make a turn toward a better day.

There is hope, and that hope for rebuilding is to be found in casting our gaze upon God amidst hard times. For any person, city, or country, the key to moving forward after disaster is in the turnaround. Turning from old ways of doing things toward new and better ways of building is the answer. The better way finds its establishment upon a solid foundation, a standard for building. Without a proper standard of measurement, there is no hope for building a meaningful future. Looking back on things in the aftermath of a catastrophe, reality becomes much clearer. Hindsight, as they say, is 20/20. *Rebuild — Turn-around —*

What is abundantly clear in the aftermath of Katrina is that city, state, and national officials could have joined forces to build more safeguards around our city. Many studies have been compiled for years attesting to the implications of a disaster stemming from a levee system constructed to withstand only a Category-Three storm. One of the more significant studies, that of the fictional "Hurricane Pam," clearly demonstrated in its findings a situation all too similar to the one subsequently experienced in New Orleans. Had the findings of the report translated into a standard of measurement for the construction of proper levees, perhaps the city could have been spared much of the flooding and overwhelming damage.

As was pointed out earlier, gold has historically functioned as the standard by which financial disaster preparedness is evaluated. There was a time when gold was the measurement of value for all currencies. That is to say, behind every paper promise (dollar bills, for example) was the reality of tangible wealth in the form of gold. In the time since we have departed from the strategy of backing dollars with gold, much debate has arisen regarding the real value of paper money. It is a debate that separates many bright minds, and the issues are complex. What is not complex or debatable is the fact that any promise of wealth, value, or truth must have something real behind it. A stable levee system must have standards backing its construction, a well-built house must have a solid foundation, and a meaningful life must be constructed by embracing standards of truth and virtue.

In times of disaster, whether the catastrophe comes in the form of nature's wrath, cancer, divorce, or emotional pain, the soul must have an anchor. To make it through, let alone grow into something better, a person must have inner strength. Such strength of soul comes not from within but from above. Individuals who turn to a secure safe haven when all around them is uncertainty find character and poise to endure wind and waves.

When everything around us is falling apart — portfolios, homes, marriages, or careers — we must have something or someone to fall back on. Jesus Christ, the historic personality and presence sent by God on our behalf, is that rock. He is the standard by which our lives are measured. If we as individuals are to experience a complete turnaround in our lives, we must surrender all other emotional, physical, financial, and personal assets to God. What we will find as we do so is a corresponding rise of value in the development of our soul.

Just as gold rises in value when paper assets are in decline, the value of human life ascends to heights unknown when all confidence and trust is placed in God's hands. The return on a life well lived far exceeds the value of any amassing of toys in this life. Despite common wisdom, he who has the most toys does not win.

As Jesus said, "For what shall it profit a man, if he shall gain the whole world, and loses his own soul?" (Matt. 16:26 KJV).

The things we thirst for apart from God, though they may appear to us as profit and gain, are in actuality poverty and loss. The worth of the soul is never measured by one's bank account. It is not only possible but ordinary to find extraordinarily rich men and women who are impoverished of soul. Not only is it common, but the scriptures tell us it is very difficult for the rich to enter the kingdom of God (Matt. 19:23-24). The difficulty lies in self-deception. With riches in hand, and fists clinched tightly, it is very difficult to reach out to others and to God.

America, the proud, rich superpower, could certainly benefit from this reminder. It is entirely possible that we could again see a day when our riches are depleted and our self-sufficiency is removed. Neither I nor anyone else wants to see such a day. However, the potential is a historic reality. Should a massive storm be headed our way, the measure of our ability to navigate such a moment will depend upon our standard of life, not our standard of living. Our standard can and must be founded upon something, someone, more secure than our current pursuits.

In New Orleans and in America, the reallocation of our spiritual wealth must begin in earnest right away. A sound spiritual plan for growth and rebuilding will enable us to pursue a turnaround that will endure. As we reallocate our spiritual portfolio, we may indeed find that our worst fears can be allayed and the blessing of God can be sent our way. He is, after all, the supreme turnaround specialist. He is the great rebuilder. He is the firm foundation upon which we build the house that endures the winds and the waves. He is the foremost gold standard for life.

Turning It Around

Turnarounds are not easy to accomplish. Ask any seasoned CEO or corporate specialist, and they will tell you horror stories about the difficulties involved in this undertaking. Likewise, ask any skilled businessman just how hard it is to save a deal that has gone sour, and you will get an earful. Take time to ask anyone who has come back from a life that has totally fallen apart, and you will wonder whether the final payoff is worth the pain endured in getting to the goal.

Ask a professional athlete about the rehabilitation required to overcome a serious injury, and you will hear tales of pain, doubt, fear, and agony. In the end, however, if you assembled all of these folks together into one focus group and asked them if the goal was worth the effort, they would all tell you they would do it all over again. When looking a turnaround square in the face, the reality can be overwhelming.

Owning up to the severity of the failures that led to the current situation can be very discouraging. This is especially true when a soul is involved. The truth must be confronted, however, and the reality of the situation must be acknowledged. This is especially difficult when it is our soul on the hot seat. God understands this truth, and He deals with us truthfully and mercifully. He does not pull any punches in addressing our shortcomings, yet He offers us hope for a renewed future. Just as any turnaround artist knows, failures must be addressed head on. That is the way God addresses us and our failures, whether as individuals or as groups. We see this fact demonstrated in the book of Jeremiah, where God, through His prophet, speaks directly to the failure of His people:

> "Woe to him who builds his house by unrighteousness, and his upper rooms by injustice, who makes his neighbor serve him for nothing and does not give him his wages, who says, 'I will build myself a great house with spacious upper rooms,' who cuts out windows for it, paneling it with cedar and painting it with vermilion.
>
> "Do you think you are a king because you compete in cedar? Did not your father eat and drink and do justice and righteousness? Then it was well with him. He judged the cause of the poor and needy; then it was well. Is not this to know me? declares the LORD.
>
> "But you have eyes and heart only for your dishonest gain,

for shedding innocent blood, and for practicing oppression and violence. . . ."

"I spoke to you in your prosperity, but you said, 'I will not listen.' This has been your way from your youth, that you have not obeyed my voice. The wind shall shepherd all your shepherds, and your lovers shall go into captivity; then you will be ashamed and confounded because of all your evil. O inhabitant of Lebanon, nested among the cedars, how you will be pitied when pangs come upon you, pain as of a woman in labor!" (Jer. 22:13-17, 21-23)

This truth directed at the nation of Israel, I must confess, sounds eerily similar to life in America today. It is a reality we must own up to if we are to begin the turnaround necessary to reconstruct our lives and souls.

We have no choice but to turn from social injustice, economic oppression, dishonest gain, and selfish pursuits. God instructs us about the state of our future if we do not begin the turnaround. In Amos, we read of God's repeated warnings meant to serve as the loving rod of discipline to turn His children around and save them from disaster:

"I gave you cleanness of teeth in all your cities, and lack of bread in all your places, yet you did not return to me," declares the LORD.

"I also withheld the rain from you when there were yet three months to the harvest; I would send rain on one city, and send no rain on another city; one field would have rain, and the field on which it did not rain would wither; so two or three cities would wander to another city to drink water, and would not be satisfied; yet you did not return to me," declares the LORD.

"I struck you with blight and mildew; your many gardens and your vineyards, your fig trees and your olive trees the locust devoured; yet you did not return to me," declares the LORD.

"I sent among you a pestilence after the manner of Egypt; I killed your young men with the sword, and carried away your horses, and I made the stench of your camp go up into your nostrils; yet you did not return to me," declares the LORD.

> "I overthrew some of you, as when God overthrew Sodom
> and Gomorrah, and you were as a brand plucked out of the
> burning; yet you did not return to me," declares the LORD.
> "Therefore thus I will do to you, O Israel; because I will
> do this to you, prepare to meet your God, O Israel!" (Amos
> 4:6-12)

Again, I fear, literally, this description of Israel long ago is all too similar to the city of New Orleans particularly and our nation as a whole. We must turn back, return to God. The warnings have come, the winds have blown, the waters have risen, but are we listening? Are we making the turn? If we do return, we will find a God full of mercy, grace, and compassion. Far greater is His way compared to our waywardness. He does not wish to flood us with His wrath; rather He longs to come to our aid and stand with us in our struggle to rebuild our lives. We must see the heights from which we have fallen and look up for help if we are to be restored. The Gospel of John speaks of God's desire and ability to turn things all around.

Chapter 8 of John's book tells the story of a woman caught in adultery. Apparently, religious leaders had been made aware of the dishonorable character of a loose woman. It appears from reading the text that the leaders then set out to catch her in the act, expose her, and bring her to justice. The woman, in actuality, was merely a pawn in the leaders' scheme to put Jesus and His teachings to the test. Upon bringing this woman of ill repute to Jesus, the leaders pointed out that the Law of Moses demanded she be stoned for her adulterous offenses. "What shall we do?" they asked Jesus.

With creativity, brilliance, grace, and knowledge of all souls involved, Jesus turned the tables on the hypocritical interests of the religious leaders. The text tells us that at that moment Jesus bent down to write in the sand with His finger. After scribbling a few things with His finger, Jesus stood up, looked the spiritual gurus in the eyes, and said, "Let him who is without sin among you be the first to throw a stone at her" (v. 7). How marvelous!

My best guess is that Jesus had probably just listed in the sand a number of sin categories that struck directly to the hearts of the accusers. He had turned the tables on this woman's disaster by focusing the attention on her critics. As they stood stunned and silent, Jesus bent down to write again.

The text says that with the oldest first, they began to leave one by one. Was Jesus continuing the onslaught of their corrupt hearts by revealing the sins of each as He wrote in the sand? Is it not true that the longer we live, the older we get, the more aware we become of our own sinfulness?

Eventually, the scripture tells us, just Jesus and the woman were left standing together. All the accusers had scattered in stunned silence and bewilderment. Jesus said to her, "Woman, where are they? Has no one condemned you?" (v. 10). Can you hear the dry, profound humor and razor-sharp spiritual insight? It was as if He were saying, "Oh my, what a surprise, they are all gone; what a shocker! Who is left to condemn you?" The woman responded, "No one, Lord" (v. 11). She immediately recognized that the Lord of glory was dealing with her soul. And Jesus responded to her recognition of His lordship by saying, "Neither do I condemn you; go, and from now on sin no more" (v. 11). And with those words, the turnaround begins, and a new life is underway.

Notice that Jesus' desire is for good and not destruction. This woman, who by law could have been finally destroyed, was given another opportunity to rebuild her life. Jesus did not offer her an easy faith, for He told her to go and sin no more. He did, however, turn her life around for good. He desires to do the same for us— for our souls, our cities, and our nation. We must simply turn toward Him, recognize and embrace His leadership, and lovingly respond to His offer of new life by pursuing it with a desire to "sin no more."

Rightly placed affections are His goal for us. Salvation from imminent and total devastation is His promise. A life of meaning and significance is the reward. It has been said that the problem with Christianity is not that it has been tried and found wanting, but rather that it has been found hard and left untried. If we will try it, we will find a life worth living.

The writing is on the wall, and in this case in the sand. Jesus, the turnaround artist, demonstrates the compassion of God and His good intentions for us when we turn and head back in His direction. Regardless of how desperate our situation has become, the divine CEO is able to bring us back to life. He does have a rebuilding plan for us.

The Apple of His Eye:
Steve Jobs and Apple Computers

One of the more striking examples of desperation to come from the growing body of stories in the aftermath of Katrina is that of the recently revealed "mercy killings" at a number of New Orleans hospitals. In the days following Katrina's onslaught, dealing with the sad possibility that all hope was lost, some doctors and nurses (those given the task of preserving life) made a decision to take the ultimate fate of patients into their own hands. As the story goes, rather than allowing these elderly and critically ill patients to eventually die from their sickness or from starvation, the "caregivers" decided the merciful thing to do would be to "help" them die, and quickly. In stark contrast to the heroic rescue efforts that went on for days and days throughout the city, the leadership in these hospitals, or so it appears, chose ease and expediency over hope and heroism.

Again, I call our attention to the implications of the agenda in America for legalizing any ultimate "choices" we as humans wish to make. Were these acts in keeping with the oath doctors take upon receiving their commission to administer hope and healing to those with whom they come in contact? Who is to say what good may have come from the remaining days of life any of these patients may have had? Who determined it was their right to choose death for these patients? How will the families of these now deceased loved ones respond? Where do we draw the line in

America? At what point is life valuable? Who determines what makes a life valuable? And who is to say, as desperate as things may get, that all is lost and without hope?

Steve Jobs, the legendary CEO of Apple Computers, and college dropout, is a case study in the value of never quitting, never giving in when all appears lost. The story of Apple is one that demonstrates the value of viewing the original goal, passion, and mission as something to cling to until the very end.

Steve Jobs is a huge figure in the world of computers and wealth building. He cofounded Apple, gave the world its first PC-like machine in 1976, was a multimillionaire before the age of thirty, and was the prime mover behind Apple's early and rapid success. Bored, burned out, or just looking for something else to do, Jobs walked away from his company.

Upon Jobs' departure from the company in the mid-eighties, Apple began to flounder in the absence of its leader. For many years, the health of this great company was deteriorating. With market share plummeting, profits falling, on the verge of terminal illness, and with all the experts pronouncing impending doom, Steve Jobs came back to Apple in 1997 as the "interim CEO." In 2000, he officially took the helm as the point man and CEO of this dying company. When nearly everyone else had given up hope, Steve Jobs found inspiration in the initial passion and mission that had birthed this once-great company, and he committed himself to a major rebuilding effort.

His first step toward recovering what had been lost, and in moving forward to making it better than ever, was to give the company a complete makeover. Apple, Jobs was convinced, had to be a company of fresh vision and forward thinking. Jobs was determined to demonstrate that this dying behemoth could and would lead the industry once again. He started the makeover by totally redesigning the company and its products from the ground up. The image, marketing, and design had to be new, fresh, out of the box, and beyond anything the industry had ever seen. The "Think Differently" marketing campaign set the tone for Apple's new future.

In the days following his return, and still today, the compelling artistry, design, and user-friendliness have seemingly everyone craving Apple products once again. The new highly stylized computers, the iPod, the new Nano, iTunes, and the software have developed a cult-like following. Though I cranked out this manuscript on a Windows-based laptop, in my home office there sits one fantastic Apple desktop with a ridiculously large Apple cinema screen. Somewhere in the house are a couple of Apple iPods. This company's alluring products are so inspiringly designed and artistically styled that they elicit a feverish response from consumers. The attraction is back at Apple, market share is increasing, profits are climbing, and our culture is eating up its products like candy. The turnaround is happening. The company is better than ever. The future looks bright.

How does this kind of thing take place? What is it that enables a once-faltering and sputtering entity to come back to life in such a manner? We have heard it quoted many times, "Never, ever, ever, ever, ever, ever, ever give up. Never give up. Never give up. Never give up." These often misquoted words of Winston Churchill are used by speakers, writers, and self-help gurus around the world regularly. What many of us are unaware of, however, is the occasion, context, and body of the entire speech.

Context means everything if a given quotation is to really speak its truth. The rousing speech, given by Churchill amidst the battles raging in World War II, is a testament to our call to persevere and press through the darkest of days. The speech, made to students at the Harrow School, conveys strength, character, poise, and resolve to fight for that which one considers to be of ultimate value. Those words, in their entirety, have many parallels to the issues addressed in this book. For our purpose here we will look at a few of those inspiring words in their context.

Britain, the apple of Winston Churchill's eye, was worth fighting for even amidst his country's darkest days. His words have impacted many throughout history. In that now famous speech he stated:

> The ten months that have passed have seen very terrible, catastrophic events in the world — ups and downs, misfortunes — but can anyone sitting here this afternoon, this October afternoon, not feel deeply thankful for what has happened in the time that has passed and for the very great improvement in the position of our country and of our home? . . . Surely from this period of ten months, this is the lesson: Never give in. Never give in. (The Churchill Centre)

Great accomplishment and great leadership each begin with courage and resolve. Likewise, strength for the storms of life is derived from an unflinching commitment to fight until the end for God's purposes. The battles may seem overwhelming and the enemies often present a formidable front. Yet, we must never quit. The enemy, the storm, the winds and waves, do not have the ability to defeat those who rely upon the great power of our God. Churchill's famous words are appropriate, "Never, never, never, never — in nothing, great or small, large or petty — never give in, except to convictions of honor and good sense. Never yield to force. Never yield to the apparently overwhelming might of the enemy."

And so, the call to fight for that which is important to us must be heard loud and clear. Rather than giving in amidst life's most desperate moments and pronouncing a death sentence upon all of our dreams, we must passionately pursue that which is so precious to us. Never give up, never give in, never give out. Never quit pursuing your God-given passion. No matter where you are in the journey, at the top of the heap or beneath the rubble, turn your gaze upward. Think differently, think with the mind of Christ, and go for it. Attempt the ridiculous for the good of others as God inspires you. If you think your idea, your dream, your passion to rebuild your life is just too hard or too unthinkable, read the story of Bill Bowerman and the creation of the first Nike tennis shoe. Pour the rubber into the waffle iron, cut the mold, build the shoe, lace it up, and go for it. *Just do it!* God tells us we are the apple of his eye (Ps. 17:8). He assures us of His love for us, and He has told us over and over again that He is about the business of rebuilding. His ways are not our ways, His thinking is outside the box, and life looks much different from His perspective. Although everything around us may appear to be death and destruction, through God's eyes the view is much better. From the grave He brings new life, fresh dreams, and bright futures. In His hands, devastation and hopelessness are transformed into life, and that abundantly (John 10:10). Pick up a hammer; it's time to start rebuilding!

Hope from the Grave: Lazarus

"It's just too late, too far gone, too complicated, too ugly, and too hopeless." "There is too much water under the bridge." "I give up." Those words and others like them are spoken every day by far too many people caught in the grip of disaster. The death of a dream, a home, a family, a romantic relationship, or a life can be deflating. We have all, no doubt, experienced moments when we have thrown up our hands and in sheer exhaustion said, "That's it; I'm done."

Jesus was and is familiar with this reality, and He is able to meet us in those moments and offer us hope. He does not ignore our tears or command that we pick ourselves up by our own boot-straps. Rather, the scriptures tell us that God bottles up all of our tears (Ps. 56:8) and feels our pain. He sees, He knows, He is aware of our predicament, and He responds. His response is always on time, and He is always near, even when we think He is far off (Heb. 13:5).

The smell of death lingered in New Orleans long after Katrina picked up her bags and moved on. She came in hell-bent on bringing down the city, and in her coming and going she left her mark. The scent of rotting and decaying food (some 250,000 refrigerators filled with spoiled food lined the streets for many weeks), animal carcasses, and decomposing bodies drifted on the New Orleans air for months. It is a smell unlike anything one could imagine. Weeks after the storm, evacuees who came back to assess damage did so with masks strapped to their faces and gloves on their hands. The stench was too much to handle.

Jesus knows something of this deadly stench. He is familiar with the sights, smells, and pain of death. The story of Lazarus in John 11:1-44 shows us just how touched the Lover of our souls is by the sting of death.

Mary and Martha, who were friends of Jesus, were troubled by the severe illness of their brother Lazarus. Knowing of Jesus' love for Lazarus, the women sent a message to Jesus to inform Him of the illness. Although He was aware of Lazarus' sickness, Jesus stayed where He was for two full days. At the end of that time, He told His disciples that His friend Lazarus had died.

Then Jesus and the disciples headed back to be with those grieving the loss. Mary and Martha were deeply troubled and in tremendous grief. The sisters had lost their brother, and they could not understand why Jesus had not come to be with them during this difficult time. Upon His arrival, Martha went to Jesus first and said, "Lord, if you had been here, my brother would not have died" (v. 21).

Jesus' response to Martha was intended to give hint to the wonder about to be performed, but Martha could not see through the grief. Jesus replied, "Your brother will rise again. . . . I am the resurrection and the life. Whoever believes in me, though he die, yet shall he live, and everyone who lives and believes in me shall never die. Do you believe this?" (vv. 23, 25-26). Martha's reply was something along the lines of, "Yes, Jesus, I know that in heaven we will all live forever." Theology, however, as we all know, is only comforting to a point.

At times like this, we need a tangible touch from God. This is probably what Martha was thinking at this moment. After this theological exchange, Martha went to find Mary and tell her of Jesus' whereabouts. Mary came to Jesus, weeping along with other mourners. The account tells us that as she came to Jesus, she fell at his feet mourning and weeping, saying, "Lord, if you had been here, my brother would not have died" (v. 32). Jesus had heard this statement before. Mary and Martha's feelings were much like ours in such moments. Seeing Jesus work miracles in the lives of others, and knowing of His ability to change our world with just one word, we often wonder, "Why does He not do something for me?"

As the account unfolds, we see that Jesus was touched deeply by the pain of His friends and by the loss of Lazarus. He asked them, "Where have you laid him?" (v. 34). Still not getting the hint of the miracle about to overwhelm them, some in the crowd of mourners began to question Jesus' compassion and ability, "Could not he who opened the eyes of the blind man also have kept this man from dying?" (v. 37). Jesus would see this kind of doubting as He was being crucified upon the cross accomplishing the greatest victory in the history of the world. Apparently Jesus never concerned Himself with the assumptions of onlookers. Appearing to many to be always down, He was never defeated.

Jesus, we are told, was deeply moved at this point, and He wept (vv. 33-35). The One who bottles all of our tears and counts each tear that falls upon our cheeks weeps with us. He is not too detached to be touched by our humanity (Heb. 4:15). We often view God as some distant power far removed from our human realities and certainly above and beyond the concerns of our daily lives.

Too often we make the unconscious assumption that we could not possibly approach God with our questions, fears, doubts, and depression. After all, if He exists, then He must be perfect, so how could He possibly understand? He is above all of this. He expects us to pull ourselves together, put on a good face, and move on.

Jesus, however, shows us a different side of God in this encounter. This man, the perfect man, God in the flesh, clearly experiences our pain and is moved by it. In so doing, He owns our pain.

> Then Jesus, deeply moved again, came to the tomb. It was a cave, and a stone lay against it. Jesus said, "Take away the stone." Martha, sister of the dead man, said to him, "Lord, by this time there will be an odor, for he has been dead four days." (vv. 38-39)

Notice the contrast. Mary, Martha, and the onlookers feared the stench of death. Jesus, on the other hand, recognizing the reality of the odor and its implications, stared the challenge in the face and rose to meet it head on. After looking upward to the heavens and saying a few things to God, Jesus turned His gaze to the tomb and with passion and divinely empowered unction, in a loud voice commanded, "Lazarus, come out" (v. 43).

In an instant, hope sprang eternal from the grave! With grave clothes still encumbering him, Lazarus, the friend of Jesus, brother of the grieving women, came forth from the stench and darkness of death into the glorious brilliance of new life and into the light of a new day. Jesus, totally poised, yet perhaps still with tears rolling down His face, looked in the direction of the astonished onlookers and directed them, "Unbind him, and let him go" (v. 44). For anyone within sight or earshot of this wonderful event, life would never be the same again!

Karl Barth, in a very important work entitled *The Humanity of God* points to the ecstatic reality that God, in all of His divinity and "otherness," is also near. Barth instructs us that God is not remote, far removed from our pain, confusion, and destruction. Jesus demonstrated this reality in His interaction with Lazarus, Martha, and Mary. Amidst our desolation, pain, and exhaustion, God's hand is extended through the clouds, reaching us, and bottling our tears. God is for us. He has not left us all alone. Barth writes:

> God's deity is thus no prison in which He can exist only in and for Himself. It is rather His freedom to be in and for Himself but also with and for us, to assert but also to sacrifice Himself, to be wholly exalted but also completely humble, not only almighty but also almighty mercy, not only Lord but also servant, not only judge but also Himself the judged, not only man's eternal king but also his brother in time.

God, Jehovah, the Great I Am, the Alpha and Omega, the Beginning and the End, chooses to identify with us in our pain! In Jesus, He is Emmanuel, God with us amidst the storm! In His very character, in His deity, He is yet our brother in pain, adversity, and loss. This is our God.

No matter how low we may find ourselves, no matter how bad our situation may look, no matter how dead we may seem, no matter how bad the stench may be, God is able. He is able to bring hope from the grave, and He is able to rebuild the soul of any man, woman, boy, girl, city, hamlet, county, state, or nation. He is still near, and He longs to say that word again, "Unbind." In one word, He can turn death upside down. In one word, He can turn our lives right side up. In one word, He can change things. As the great hymn tells us, He is our hope and our help. Martin Luther penned the powerful and profound words long ago, yet they are still sound today. He is still, "O God, our help in ages past, our hope for years to come, our shelter from the stormy blast, and our eternal home!"

PART THREE

TIME FOR A CHANGE— REBUILDING FOR A BETTER FUTURE

A rising tide lifts all boats.

—John F. Kennedy

God of Wind and Water

Wind and water are, of course, elements without which we cannot live. The two are capable of refreshing and sustaining us, and are essential to life on our planet. Agencies, governments, and all kinds of groups are devoted to the critical task of making sure that the quality of our air and water are maintained. Technology, money, and many resources are dedicated to the management of these most basic of elements. Water treatment plants, bottled water, flavored water, spring water, well water, water testing, water parks, watering holes, water sports — there are references to the importance of water all around us.

The same is true of wind. Windmills, whirlwinds, the "Windy City," winds of change — wind is everywhere. Water provides hydration for our bodies, nourishment for plants, a habitat for sea creatures, and the backbone of the farming industry. Wind provides for our needs in similar ways that affect our use of power, the way we travel, the development of plant growth, and the balance of our environment.

Meteorologists study the trends and movement of our planet's winds and waters, and in so doing have learned much about the way our world is affected by these elements. All of us tune in regularly to hear the latest forecast for our area from the weather "experts." Though the experts are regularly proved wrong, we have come to place a great deal of confidence in them. Those of us who live in areas regularly affected by hurricanes have come to invest an extraordinary dependence on the experts during the six months of the year we have come to know as hurricane season. Some of us border on Weather Channel addiction.

Weather is all around us, and the wind and water of our world determine so much in terms of how we live from day to day. The changes brought by wind and water can and do affect our coming and going. Farmers know the importance of the right balance of wind and water, and just how important this balance is to economic survival. Sailing enthusiasts know how the wind and water can determine a great outing or a day of misery on the boat. Skiers are keenly aware of just how miserable it can be to get caught ten thousand feet up on a mountainside with the winds howling and the snow blowing. Skiing in blizzard conditions is not much fun, I can attest to that. Wind-driven snow can turn a vacation into what literally feels like a cold day in hell. Residents in areas prone to mudslides can tell of the destruction that comes from an overabundance of rain.

With so much forecasting of wind and water on the Weather Channel, CNN, and our local news stations, we can easily deceive ourselves into thinking that in our modern, technological, and "advanced" age, we can manage the effect of these elements upon our lives. However, what Katrina, the perennial wildfires in California, the mudslides in Central America, and the recent earthquakes in Asia have demonstrated is the fact that man is virtually powerless against a host of natural disasters. This far into the "advancement" of our world, we are still susceptible to the winds of change and the waters of life.

We would do well, however, to remember the origin of the winds and the waters. Rather than speaking of "Mother Nature," as do many of the meteorologists, we should consider what the scriptures say of "Father God" and His direct and personal involvement in the direction of the laws of nature. From the beginning, we see the significance of these most crucial of elements in God's plan:

> In the beginning, God created the heavens and the earth. The earth was without form and void, and darkness was over the face of the deep. And the Spirit of God was hovering over the face of the waters. . . .
> And God said, "Let there be an expanse in the midst of the waters, and let it separate the waters from waters." And God made the expanse and separated the waters that were under the expanse from the waters that were above the expanse. . . .
> And God said, "Let the waters under the heavens be gathered together into one place, and let the dry land appear." (Gen. 1:1-2, 6-7, 9)

Early on, water was instrumental in the plan of God. When the world was "without form," the waters were used to bring form to our world. Could it be that God still uses the waters and the winds to bring form to our lives? Could it be that God brings seasons of change into our world and into our lives to birth newness of vision, growth, and purpose? Just as God did with Noah, He still uses the waters to bring new beginnings when His plan has gone awry (Gen. 6-9).

Likewise, just as it was with Noah, though everyone around may doubt the sanity of those who embrace the coming storm and even question the reality of its existence, God still calls His people to see, embrace, and prepare for the rising waters to come. While God promised never to send a flood that would destroy the entire world again (Gen. 9:8-17), He certainly uses the waters and the winds to bring climate changes in our lives in order that His objectives and dreams might be accomplished.

The scriptures and history are replete with examples of God doing this very thing. For those who find shelter in Him amidst the winds and the floods, good comes from the storms. Even in being uprooted, relocated, and displaced, the purposes of God are not thwarted. In fact, God's best may be unfolding even as we find ourselves being blown away from our moorings by the winds and deposited elsewhere by the waters. Though we as people are habitually resistant to major changes in our life, in allowing God to change our view, we will find that He has lifted us to new places designed for our good. Remember, He has told us, "I have plans for you!" (Jer. 29:11).

Change Agents

In corporate America, the mastery of change has become an entire field of study. "Change agents" are those who have established themselves as gurus of corporate change. These sages of shifting realities are paid enormous sums for their insights. Change agents in the workplace are assigned the task of preparing companies for high-octane performance in a world that has one constant—change. The lifeblood of thriving companies is increasingly dependent upon their ability to change and adapt to an ever-adjusting marketplace.

Consumer trends, new technology, new methods of obtaining feedback, global economic shifts, changes in price-to-earnings ratios, paradigm shifts, and other unexpected realities make it mandatory for business leaders to excel in the management of change. If a business cannot make quick changes, it is sunk. It is no longer acceptable, we are told, for a major market player to turn slowly like a big ship. The leader must be able to develop a company that is nimble, decisive, and fast moving. Anything less will bring about a dramatic capsizing and sinking. As one leadership and business periodical recently proclaimed on its cover, businesses must "Change or Die" (*Fast Company*, May 2005).

As critical as the mastery of change is in the business world, it is far more critical when it comes to making significant and lasting changes within our souls. Change agents in the world of big business are paid so much money because their role is so critically important to success. Experts on change measures are a must for big companies who have so much at risk. Beyond the salaries and consulting fees paid to these gurus are enormous budgets for implementing the change strategies.

But there is a problem. Scientists inform us that regardless of the money spent, time allocated, and incentives given, 90 percent of people find it very hard to make lasting change in their lives. That's why, more often than not, a massive shaking must take place before most of us will consider moving toward our own change measures.

There's another big problem. Scientists tell us that even with a major crisis lending incentive, 90 percent of people will not make a much-needed change in their lifestyle. As the feature article "Change or Die," cited above, informs us, leading scientists have noted that even amidst one of life's most serious crises—a serious health problem—only a fraction of individuals will be sparked to effect a major lifestyle change.

Even most heart bypass patients, with the real potential of life-ending problems, will not change their habits following surgery. And as many CEOs and academic professionals who study change will attest, the biggest challenge to changing an organization is not the development of strategy, but rather getting people to actually change, even those who sign on to the change measures in principle.

I have watched and grieved over the choices of people close to me. Watching a friend or family member continue in some habit that is wrecking his or her body, mind, or soul is a troubling ordeal. I have seen family members, amidst the storm of lung cancer, continue to smoke. I have witnessed others close to me amidst the storm of physical, emotional, and relational brokenness continue in patterns and addictions that ultimately tore entire families apart. Too often, appeals to reason, common sense, and spiritual wisdom fell on deaf ears. It seems so hard for us to change.

It is interesting that much of the research coming from various fields of study in regard to change behavior reveals that change typically takes places only when individuals "see" life through a different lens at some point. A change of one's worldview or a reframing of one's understanding of reality is usually necessary for meaningful and lasting change to take place. Such a shift in perspective, some researchers suggest, comes through an evaluation and acceptance of the changes being considered on a multiplicity of levels — physical, emotional, intellectual, spiritual, and otherwise. A strict appeal to reason alone, as we witnessed earlier with John Donne when he asks God to "Batter my heart" is typically not sufficient. This is why the best communicators and the most effective change agents appeal to both head and heart. The implications for change in society and within the church are intriguing and will be considered in later chapters.

God has many change agents at His disposal. His measures for change come riding on the winds and waves of many different storms in our lives. If we are willing to see life through His eyes, lasting change can and will be effected in us. Just as in the world of fine art, the way we perceive an important work is often greatly affected by the framing of the piece, so too in our lives, the framing of our understanding determines what life looks like from deep inside our souls. If we are to view the rebuilding of our lives through eyes of faith, we must understand that God is at work and is unfolding His plan amidst the massive changes we may be facing. God often uses sudden and dramatic moments of upheaval in our lives to bring about lasting change in us and in others.

Interestingly, current research demonstrates that the common strategy of making change slowly does not work. Most often, it is more likely that lasting change comes about through massive and aggressive alterations. God uses disaster to present us with windows of opportunity or moments of life transformation. The faithful acceptance of life's disasters as opportunities for God to do something miraculous often leads to a change for good. Turning away from life's challenges leads to stagnation and a shrinking of the soul. Whether in the business world or in the Christian life, the "bottom line" is simple: "Change or die." (For an interesting read on developments in neuroscience and current thinking on behavioral change, see Alan Deutschman's complete article by this title in the May 2005 issue of *Fast Company* magazine.)

Now let's turn our attention to some stories of change, renewal, and redirection, and find hope in what God may be up to as He uses the winds and the waters to begin turning us toward His agenda for our lives.

The Change You've Always Dreamed Of: Martin Luther King Jr.

Martin Luther King Jr. lived a dream life. It sounds odd, perhaps, but it is true. Though his life was cut short, this king of oratory lived his life calling for a better dream in America. His was one of the most important voices in the history of our nation, and his legacy lives on forever. It was not an easy dream or an easy life to follow, but it was a life well lived. His was a life calling for radical change. In keeping with much of the research on change, many

Americans did not want to change, and the change did not come easy. Eventually, however, the change did come.

We have all seen the world through a different frame as a result of Dr. King's life and his passionate speeches, and the course of our nation's story has been altered for the better because he was willing to be a change agent. Dr. King's life and words offered us the opportunity and encouragement to embrace a new worldview.

In the pages ahead we are going to take a close look at the principles behind these powerful words. We have all heard the famous passages from Dr. King's "I have a dream" speech. But another of his speeches, which is lesser known, gives us a look at the foundation for his dream speech and dream life.

The night before his death, in his "I've been to the mountaintop" speech, Dr. King concluded his discourse with remarkable power and eloquence. Those historic words, hauntingly prophetic, still ring true today regardless of the battles that rage around us or within us. They are important for their depth of spiritual courage and for their crystal-clear divine perspective. These words, representative of the life he pursued and the dream that captivated him, are rich with many lessons that offer us insight as to how we are to make change and initiate our course of action for living the "dream life."

The essence of the message and the power of Dr. King's words, and the lessons of his life, are what we will explore together in the next few pages. The "mountaintop" speech is remarkable, and it is worth taking the time to read it in its entirety. At this time, however, our purpose is to look at the essence of this message, which is distilled in one passage from the speech. This one passage, in reality, is the summation of all of Dr. King's speeches and the force behind his dream life. It all comes down to this one thought.

In the "mountaintop" speech he said, "I don't know what will happen now. . . . It doesn't matter. . . . Mine eyes have seen the glory of the Lord."

In these words we find the central life theme of Dr. Martin Luther King Jr. Seeing God makes all the difference. It is true for all of us. None of us is promised a rosy future and complete bliss in this life. Yet, knowledge of the One who gives us life, and the ability to see Him as He is, secures our souls and shores up our hearts. All of life looks different once we see the Creator for who He is. From this vision, all other visions flow. From this central truth, several lessons spring up from the life of Dr. King.

Lessons from a Dream Life

(1) Once we have seen the glory of the Lord, then, and only then, does life come into proper perspective.

Dr. King's inspiring words, spoken the night before his death, and the focus of his life, testify to his lack of fear in the face of those who would seek to do him harm. Dr. King's focus enabled him to speak of his lack of concern for his own well being. Because he had seen "the glory of the Lord," everything else paled in significance. In light of the knowledge of God, we see ourselves as we are, we see the majesty of our Creator, and we recognize the futility of all that does not derive its meaning and purpose from Him. If we are to have any power for change, it must come from outside of ourselves. Change, as the researchers point out, is very unlikely for the majority of us. Enabled, however, by a power beyond ourselves, change is attainable.

(2) When we are living for a purpose bigger than ourselves, the dream becomes the "the thing."

Even our own lives seem dispensable for the cause. The thought of death, while real, does not deter us from our passion for the fulfillment of the dream. Many in New Orleans and the surrounding areas are contemplating a new dream for the city. The unfortunate reality, however, is that most are beginning to call for a "life-as-usual" approach. The dream seems to be a desire to get back to the way things used to be. If we can embrace a dream beyond "normal," beyond "the way it used to be," then we can find passion for a pursuit worthy of our time, effort, and sacrifice. There does appear to be a great deal of rhetoric flying around about building New Orleans bigger and better, yet the outworking of that rhetoric is not quite living up to the dream at this point.

(3) One glimpse of the mountaintop is enough to convince us of the sufficiency of the Dream-giver, the One who actually created the mountain.

He, the Creator, becomes our all in all. From the mountaintop, everything else looks so small. If we can gain a fresh understanding of God's agenda for the human community, we will be on our way to building our cities and our nation better than ever. The Maker of the mountain has a dream for our communities that provides for economic opportunity, educational enhancement, vibrant social initiatives, care for the poor and needy, and spiritual revitalization. With a holistic approach to rebuilding that is pointed toward the building of soul and structures, we have a much greater chance for success. Change research points out this fact as well.

(4) Quality trumps quantity.

Dr. King's words remind us of this countercultural truth. As an investment broker of rare collectible assets, I have always told my clients that quality rather than quantity of assets should be the goal. Dr. King understood that this principle was true of life. Longevity was not the ultimate aim; rather, the quest of the dream determined his essence. To live well is the goal. To build well should be our goal. As we look toward rebuilding our cities and our lives, we must begin the process with an acknowledgment that quality of rebuilding is what counts. Some will suggest that we should rebuild everything. The reality is that a more strategic approach should be embraced with an eye toward improving the quality of those parts of New Orleans that really ought to be rebuilt.

(5) When we know that the "Promised Land" is secured in the future, worry and fear diminish.

The knowledge that the ultimate dream will at some point be fulfilled is the soul's anchor amidst any storm. Like Moses and so many others, Dr. King found his strength in the promise of victory ahead. The knowledge that the dream life we are building is a God-given vision assures us of the outcome. Some are called to see the promise fulfilled here on earth; some, like Dr. King, are called to proclaim the dream and empower others to pursue it after they are gone. In the end, the victory is for all. Knowing that God is smiling upon the building of our life settles our soul and gives grace amidst all obstacles that may come. Nothing can stop the man or woman, boy or girl, who is pursuing God's call for the future.

(6) The desire to do the Lord's will is enough.

Dr. King continually offered his listeners insight into the unfailing force behind his fight, the only true passion that ever holds up amidst the storms of life, and the only hope for our future: God's will—nothing more, nothing less.

The Westminster Confession tells us of the ultimate issue: to know God and enjoy Him forever. The two go hand in hand. Those who know Him enjoy Him. He really does give life, and life abundantly. We tend to get caught up in the world's agenda for obtaining happiness. The message given us by the world is that the pursuit of toys and pleasure is the road to happiness. In reality, these pursuits distract us and hinder us from obtaining the life God has planned and intended for us from the beginning.

In exchange for the temporary enticements and allurements of this world, God offers us peace, contentment, and an internal life that apart from Him we can never know. That is why no matter how high we may climb the ladder of success or how much money we may make, we will never be at rest apart from a knowledge of God. Saint Augustine once wrote that our souls were created with a God-given void. In that place, a place only God can fill, He offers to place His Spirit. We will have no rest, said Augustine, until we find our rest in God.

(7) If the dream is God-given, it must be pursued.

Here is the summation of Dr. King's life and his legacy. This is the essence of a life worth living. As was the case for the nation of Israel in the Old Testament, the life God calls us to is the only option if we want a sustainable future. To turn from God's agenda for our life personally, as a city, as a nation, leads only to more misery. If we are to rebuild with the promise of a hopeful future, we must build according to His plan. In stark contrast to the lives of those already rebuilding the "old way," we must pursue a new future.

It is sad to hear that the first businesses reopened in New Orleans were the strip clubs. Equally disturbing are calls for the city to embrace an expanded gambling district in New Orleans in an effort to "jump start" the economy. In a city notorious for crime, filth, immorality, drunkenness, and dirty politics, an embrace of an industry leading to more of the same is not the answer. If we fail to understand that a different way is best for our future, and if we miss God's call for change, we are in for more destruction.

It is incongruous for leaders to call for the help of the church amidst disaster, and then turn from God's message for life building and community forming once the panic has subsided. Similarly, those caught in the violent storms of life as a result of bad decisions cannot call on God and claim His name while pursuing the very activities that have led to their demise. His plan, His way, is the only way. The very pursuit of His plan is what will bring us fulfillment, purpose, poise, and passion — things we all crave. Dr. King's speeches were characterized by a call for change and by a life filled with the values he espoused, and his call for change in America was eventually heard. Change is possible. A change for good is preferable. God offers us the means for change.

In the aftermath of Hurricane Katrina, our nation has become aware of the depth of the storm that still rages in our country regarding race and class. The looting, desperation, and revelations of the extent of poverty in one of America's most-visited cities gave onlookers a tragic look at how much change is still needed in this country. The changes we must pursue will not come overnight, and they will require a radical approach. In the end, however, these changes offer us a much brighter future. The changes accomplished through the efforts of Dr. King came at a great price, but the goal and the achievements were worth the struggle. All the difficulty, pain, loss, and sacrifice paid off in the long run. Our nation, as a result of the extreme changes called for in the battle for civil rights, is stronger, more diverse, and much richer.

The changes to which God calls us are always for our good. At times those changes require that we go through intense turmoil and loss. What we lose in the exchange, however, is always returned with much greater reward. When we move from the slavery of brokenness, division, and spiritual poverty, into the light of healing, community, and integrity, we always win. In the wake of disaster and displacement, God's desire is to bring radical change into our lives. This change in values, priorities, location, profession, goals, and relationships will result in a future we could not have imagined.

Washed Away:
John Coltrane — A Love Supreme

John Coltrane was a jazz master, but his accomplishments reached beyond the realm of jazz, and today his recordings are still studied by musicians of every stripe. If you have ever taken time to listen to his work, you know what it is to be washed away, lost for a time. "Trane," as he came to be known, pushed the envelope in the jazz world. Always looking for a fresh sound, an innovative creation, Coltrane was, perhaps, the hinge point for change in the jazz world. His music registers on a different scale from the many jazz greats who had gone before or who have come since.

Coltrane's mastery of the saxophone is legendary, as is his ability to carry listeners beyond what they have known or experienced. Trane's greatest achievement as a musician is the highly regarded "A Love Supreme." He knew almost immediately that it was what his entire musical journey was leading up to.

He had come to know also how far away he was from truly living life with passion, understanding, and insight. Leading up to the creation of this work, Coltrane's story was like too many we have heard. Fame, travel, money, and the pursuit of pleasure had all led to a life of addiction and desperation. As the winds blew over the years, the storm within his soul grew in intensity. Eventually, the addictions, brokenness, and strife washed over him, and he made a turn, a change. Out of this change, one of the most important contemporary musical contributions on record was birthed. "A Love Supreme" spoke to him immediately, and it has arrested hearers every since.

"A Love Supreme" was born over a five-day period in 1964. Coltrane had been going non-stop that year and had recently seen the birth of his first son. Taking a few weeks away from his brutal schedule and planning to spend time with his wife and child, Coltrane got away from it all. He took his wife and son to their new home where he planned to "kick back" for a while. Then "the work" came calling. Amidst the joy and expectation of a newborn son, John Jr., came the birth of another creation.

This new birth would be the crowning achievement of his musical life and would demonstrate a newfound desire to leave his old life behind in pursuit of the divine call to a higher life. His new artistic creation would be a marvelous, poetic, heart-stirring jazz tribute to God. After those five days of seclusion in a separate part of the house, John Coltrane came back to earth a different man. His wife knew something different had taken place. Ashley Kahn, in the introduction to his book on John Coltrane, titled after Trane's most famous work, records Alice Coltrane's remarks, "It was like Moses coming down from the mountain, it was so beautiful. He walked down and there was that joy, that peace in his face, tranquility."

Alice goes on to speak of the "different" quality of spirit that was evident in her husband. Coltrane had written and recorded scores of music prior to this moment, but something was unique in this creation. This was an experience unlike any that had come before. Alice inquired of her husband regarding the special quality of this newfound inspiration. Coltrane simply said, "This is the first time that I have received all of the music for what I want to record, in a suite. This is the first time I have everything, everything ready."

This work, written as a tribute to God, became a best seller as soon as it hit the stores. Its impact still reaches listeners today. Musicologists, musicians, and music lovers can tell of their first encounters with this amazing work. Kahn points to a few of the memorable recollections of first-timers like Carlos Santana, who said, "The first time I heard 'A Love Supreme,' it really was an assault. It could've been from Mars as far as I was concerned, or another galaxy."

Bono, the lead singer for the megaband U2, first heard "A Love Supreme" while on tour in 1987. Sitting high above the Magnificent Mile and atop the historic Grand Hotel in Chicago, Bono was deeply struck by Trane's music. He commented, "There is so much wickedness in the world but beauty is our consolation prize . . . the beauty of John Coltrane's reedy voice, its whispers, its knowingness . . . Coltrane began to make sense to me." Just as Santana, Bono, and many others have gotten washed away to another place while listening to Coltrane's work, so we too can be carried away by the Master's purposes.

The experience of Coltrane moving on from a life of addiction and despair toward something more birthed a musical achievement that will live on for many years. His willingness to hear, listen, and respond to God stirring him, moving him, and offering him a better life provided all of us something of beauty we can appreciate. Had he chosen to stay where he was, living in what he had previously known, we would be without this great work. And the same is true of us. When we are brought to that "moment," that fork in the road, that turning point, we must pursue the route that God assures us is for an enlarging of the borders of our heart. Moving on and allowing God to wash away what we formerly knew is critical to our future.

Like Santana, though, we may not at first see the patterns in the music, but in time we can come to recognize the value of God's plan. In the wash cycle of God's work, we find a life clean, fresh, new, and more desirable. When the old is gone and the new has come, we understand what Coltrane intended in titling his glorious work "A Love Supreme." It is the Creator's supreme love that gives our lives direction. The supreme love of God is where we find a life worth living. In the stirrings of our lives, we ought to look for the hand of God seeking to lead us to a better place. Washed in the waters of His unending love, we find ourselves carried away to new life. Displacement of the life we once knew may be the very thing we need.

Getting Carried Away: Evacuating to Dallas

As I was writing these words, I was reminded of a rousing sermon I had heard a few weeks earlier. The sermon title was "I Got Carried Away." In the days immediately following Katrina, I spent a few weeks in Dallas. I have long had an appreciation for the heritage, skill, drama, and process of black preaching in America. The rhythm, timing, poetry, call and response, and use of rising crescendo all mix in a great black preacher's sermon delivery to create a form of art when done well. Martin Luther King Jr. was, perhaps, the pinnacle of the art form.

Another of the great black preachers in our country is Bishop T. D. Jakes, who leads The Potter's House in Dallas. His "I Got Carried Away" sermon, which he gave two weeks after the storm, was stirring, insightful, and compelling. It confirmed what God had already begun to birth in me. His message to the listeners that day, quite a few of them hurricane evacuees, was one of hope amidst disaster. At times, Bishop Jakes suggested, God carries us away in order to bring us to better things. When everything around us is falling apart, when life has given nothing but years of disability and pain, when the future is uncertain, God can reach in and carry us away to a better place. In disaster, loss, and displacement God is able to move us to higher ground.

When God carried me away from the city of New Orleans to Dallas, I felt prompted to use the time there to hear some of the great preachers in that town. I knew God was using that time to do something in me, but I was not sure just what He was up to. In the many waking hours, days, and weeks spent in Dallas, I kept coming back to a theme in my heart and mind, that of God's taking me and others away for a purpose. As was the case a few other times in my life, I could really sense God forming something in me. I have had many dreams and ambitions along the way, most of which have not and, perhaps, will not come to fruition, but this thing that was in me while in Dallas just seemed different.

I left the New Orleans area on the Saturday before the storm and headed to Dallas to stay with my sister and her husband. Their home would come to be an evacuee stop for a number of people displaced by the storm. Shortly after arriving there, my mother, my children, and I met an unassuming older woman who lived just two doors down. I had just come back to my sister's house after a very long day of work, and was distracted by all that was happening back home and the constant news coverage of it. I was emotionally spent.

As I walked up to the house, looking forward to settling down on the couch to get the latest news via television and my laptop, I saw Helga heading our way. Realizing she was eager to meet us, I put down my briefcase, painted on a strained smile, and greeted her. As she welcomed us, the evacuees, with open arms and a big smile, I had a distinct prompting directing me to put down my agenda, close my mouth, and listen. I just knew that this woman, whom I had never met, was going to teach me or share something with me of great value. Eventually, after Helga had welcomed us, she invited us to a Bible study she was holding in her nearby home the following evening. Little did I know then just how plainly God would meet me and reveal to me the place He had prepared for me as he carried me away from New Orleans for a time.

The next night, my mother and I were again emotionally drained and not too sure that a Bible study was the place to spend the evening, but we ventured over there nonetheless. We arrived a bit early, sat down with Helga, and God began to work. In the moments before the study, Helga told us her story, one very much like that of the world-famous Corrie ten Boom. Helga had, in fact, stood in the watch shop with Corrie in the past. Like Corrie, Helga had herself endured the brutal events surrounding the Holocaust. She told us stories of God's miraculous working to sustain her during those dark days, and it was brilliantly evident that this woman had, through great disaster, been made into a jewel of a person. During those moments before the Bible study began, God reaffirmed the sense in me that my meeting Helga was an appointment divinely directed by Him.

The study lasted about two hours but seemed like only fifteen minutes. All it amounted to was a woman of God, with wisdom deeper and more secure than I have seen just about anywhere, with a Bible on her lap telling of how God's loving hand is enough to bring us through the journeys He has for us. She spoke of abiding in Him, pursuing His plan, and turning our soul toward Him. I knew, listening to her, that she had lived it, learned it, and seen it work.

Toward the end of the study, she asked that everyone pray with her. Shortly after she began to pray, she abruptly broke stride, looked up at me, and spoke directly to me. Here I was in a city far away from home in the house of a woman I had never met, and yet she spoke directly to the huge issues that had been swarming in me for a long time. For too long, I had been looking for God's loving hand amidst the disasters of my life. In recent months, I had been asking God if He had misplaced the bottle of tears He had collected from my eyes. I was wondering if there would ever be a day in which I could truly experience some of the dreams I felt He had birthed in me.

Just as had happened while I was struggling with doubt earlier in my life, God directly reminded me of His plan for me, His plan to provide me a hope and a future. The two big questions in my heart for some time had been whether God indeed held my tears, and whether He could or would redeem His plan for me to help others come to know, understand, and follow Him.

As Helga looked up and spoke to me, she said, "God knows all your tears. He bottles them up and has counted each one. He is bringing you to a place where He will use you in unique ways to bind up wounds and bring healing to others." She went on to quote the scripture that God had been beating into me over the course of the last year and a half as I struggled with the pain of a broken marriage: "I have plans for you . . . plans for your good . . . plans to prosper you and give you a hope and a future." I was floored. At that moment, God's message was made clear to me.

He knows our plight, He feels our pain, and He carries us away for His purposes. His desire is to take us from life as normal to life abundantly lived under His gaze. He has plans for us, to prosper us and to give us a hope and a future. Looking back, that time with Helga was the beginning of the vision to write this book. The days following would bring the clarity, passion, and purpose to pursue this project.

That brings me back to Bishop T. D. Jakes and his message, "I Got Carried Away." He preached from a text, Mark 2:1-12, that describes Jesus' interaction with a man who was "sick with palsy," paralyzed, and unable to pursue the dreams pounding in his heart. As the drama unfolds, we find that the man and his friends recognized that if there was any hope, any escape from this disability, it was to be found in the person of Jesus. Hearing that Jesus was in a house nearby, the man was carried by his friends to the house only to find no way in. The crowds around Jesus were so massive that there was no way into the home. Desperate for a meeting with the Master, the men devised a plan outside of the box. Unable to get in from the ground floor, they made their way up the roof with the paralytic and improvised.

Once atop the roof, the men tore it open and lowered their friend into the house where Jesus was present. Desperate times call for desperate measures. When all hope is lost, when the illness is terminal, when the marriage is done, when the death of a sibling, friend, lover, or family member crushes the heart, when no fix is in view, only one audience will do.

Knowing this, these men took all the measures necessary to ensure a meeting with the Man who with a single word could make things new. Only in being carried away was this man able to find the One who could set things right in his life for the first time. Only in being carried away did this man find the One who did not ignore his pleas, look down upon him in disgust, and cast him aside as unusable. Only in being carried away did this man, a paralytic, find the One who could identify with his tears and meet him in his pain. Only in being carried away did this man find healing. Only in being carried away did this man perceive and receive an entirely new future.

Sometimes, we must allow God to carry us away in order to fulfill His plan for us. We must, at times, have our view of life challenged in order to have new vistas opened to us. We must, at times, have patterns of behavior that are wrecking our souls confronted in order for Him to wash away the filth that has polluted us. We must at times, be carried away from our own selfish agenda and moved toward His agenda for us. We must, at times, be carried away from conditions that hinder us from experiencing life in all its fullness in order to be carried to opportunity, purpose, and passion.

We must, at times, be carried away.

Just a couple days after being with Helga for that Bible study and processing the message given to me there, I went with my family to The Potter's House, where Bishop Jakes gave his message. I sat there with goose bumps all over me as God reaffirmed His message. Jakes' sermon was the third clarification of God's leading, as earlier that morning my family and I had attended another church out in the Dallas suburbs where the very same text was used. A week earlier, God had stirred a similar theme in me while at another church in Dallas, having heard another of America's great black preachers, Dr. Tony Evans. We will look at his message together a bit later as we deal with the church's role in our current cultural disaster.

God's call to us when the storms of life come and threaten to take everything from us is to turn to Him for rescue. Unlike the storm victims in the devastated areas in and around New Orleans who called out for help day after day, we will not have to ask who will help us. He will respond. His timing is always right, His purposes are always sure, and His plans for us are always good. Though the wind and waves may appear to have won the day and sunk our ship, we need not fear. Jesus, the Man who lives, walks upon the very waters that would threaten to overturn our lives.

In John 6:16-21 we read:

> When evening came, his disciples went down to the sea, got into a boat, and started across the sea to Capernaum. It was now dark, and Jesus had not yet come to them. The sea became rough because a strong wind was blowing. When they had rowed about three or four miles, they saw Jesus walking on the sea and coming near the boat, and they were frightened. But he said to them, "It is I, do not be afraid." Then they were glad to take him into the boat, and immediately the boat was at the land to which they were going.

He is the God of wind and water. He controls it all. Look closely at the storm in which you now find yourself. You may very well see your answer, your future, walking calmly toward you upon the water and sailing with you upon the wind. You may be nearer to your dream future than you ever imagined. The change you always wanted deep within you may be at hand. Don't go it alone; welcome Him into the boat. Let Him carry you away!

PART FOUR

BUILDING GOD'S WAY

The difference between a rut and a grave is the depth.
—Gerald Burrill

A Glimpse of the Bigger Plan

There is a great deal of talk about vision today. We hear speeches on vision at graduation ceremonies, corporate meetings, leadership conferences, church services, and seminars. Bookstore shelves are filled with volumes that address the need for vision. The question comes to mind, "What is all this vision-speak about?" Why have leaders all over the globe come to embrace the importance of seeing a desirable future?

The scriptures tell us that, "Where there is no vision, the people perish" (Prov. 29:18 KJV). Another way of putting it is, "If you don't view your life and your future from God's perspective, you are going to come to ruin." Thousands of homes and billions of dollars were lost when the New Orleans levees gave way. The huge debate in the Crescent City at this moment is about who will be sued and who is to blame for the failure of the levees. The city government, the state government, the federal government, and the Corps of Engineers all certainly share in the culpability.

For years, nearly everyone agreed that New Orleans was in dire need of a levee system that could withstand a Category-Five hurricane. The only problem was that though everyone agreed, apparently no one envisioned the potential of a hurricane of this magnitude coming through anytime soon, and so the levees were built to withstand only a Category-Three storm. The lack of clarity regarding the impending disaster has left a great city in ruins. Vision, the ability to see the future in light of all its potential and pitfalls, is supposed to translate into action that addresses the unfolding of the days ahead. Had the vision for a strong and protected New Orleans been more of a reality in the minds of leaders, perhaps we would not be in this mess.

Just as clarity of vision enables corporate CEOs, political figures, church leaders, social reformers, and anyone in leadership to accomplish great things, vision in the life of an individual is absolutely critical for building a future and for protection against the inevitable storms life will bring. Ultimate vision in life determines, ultimately, what kind of life will be lived. As has been said, "Everyone dies, but not everyone really lives." Without a proper worldview, a vision of life as it really is, our life will become a mess.

Whether we find ourselves with money, toys, fame, and success at every turn, or whether we find ourselves living in constant struggle, life away from God's vision for us will always be less than satisfying. There are those, like Mother Teresa, who lived a life with few possessions, yet a life full of the presence of God. Her years on earth inspired this generation, and will do the same for those in the future. By contrast, there are those who live life surrounded by pleasures on every hand and demonstrate to everyone looking on their depravity of soul and lack of virtue.

The examples are endless. There are also those who have little, and thirst after, crave, and covet all the things they don't have. These people seemingly cannot live with passion and joy unless the promise of abundance is on their mind every second. When the fulfillment of their desires is too long delayed or never comes, these people remain embittered and miserable. We are all aware, also, of those who have plenty, some more than plenty, and yet retain their soul and live as life as it ought to be lived. What is the difference between those who build a life worth living and those who come to ruin spiritually, emotionally, and relationally?

The answer is where we find the foundation for building a future that's worth pursuing. The answer lies in how we view life and how we see our role here on this earth. The answer is found in building our inner life upon bedrock principles given to us by our Creator. To build anything of significance down below, we must begin by gaining perspective from above.

Viewing and Building Life from the Floor Up

Isaiah was one of God's chosen oracles; he was a prophet. As a man singled out by God to give His message, he seemingly met a higher standard that few, if any, could ever reach. In the days of the

Old Testament, days in which God was held in such extreme reverence by His followers, worshippers did not even dare approach God in the most sacred of worship places. Worship customs and regulations demanded that only God's singled-out servants were to approach Him in the inner sanctum. And when these chosen few did approach God on behalf of other worshippers, they did so with a great sense of awe and humility. One would think then that these men of God were keenly aware of their spiritual superiority and insight. Surely, they had life all figured out. Every day must have been spent with great clarity, purpose, and intentionality. These great men of faith knew at every moment where they were headed. Or so we might assume.

The sixth chapter of the book of Isaiah gives us a powerful account of one of God's great spokesmen and his view of the One he served. The passage is actually a recording of Isaiah's vision of God and his response to that vision. In these verses, we find a man coming "totally unglued" before his Creator. What is so startling about the account is that this man, beyond reproach when compared to the standard of conduct in his day, and certainly in our day, seemingly grieves over his lack of ability to "measure up" before a holy God. It speaks volumes to us regarding the state of our own souls, and it certainly speaks definitively to our country and the state of our nation spiritually. Our view of goodness has fallen so far! Let's look at the text:

> In the year that King Uzziah died I saw the Lord sitting upon a throne, high and lifted up; and the train of his robe filled the temple. Above him stood the seraphim. Each had six wings: with two he covered his face, and with two he covered his feet, and with two he flew. And one called to another and said:
>
> "Holy, holy, holy is the LORD of hosts;
> the whole earth is full of his glory!"
>
> And the foundations of the thresholds shook at the voice of him who called, and the house was filled with smoke. And I said: "Woe is me! For I am lost; for I am a man of unclean lips,

and I dwell in the midst of a people of unclean lips; for my eyes have seen the King, the LORD of hosts!"

Then one of the seraphim flew to me, having in his hand a burning coal that he had taken with tongs from the altar. And he touched my mouth and said: "Behold, this has touched your lips; your guilt is taken away, and your sin atoned for." (Isa. 6:1-7)

What is happening here? How can it be that a man, a holy man, a really holy man, can have an encounter with the God he represents and just "lose" it like this? Isn't this a bit "overboard"? Is he not taking this all too seriously? Is he just a bit too carried away?

What is important to understand about this passage is the transformation taking place in Isaiah. There are times in our lives when God challenges everything we know, think, and comprehend about life. Strategically, when we think we have it all figured out, God shows us we do not. Just as the apostle Paul got knocked off his "high horse," so too Isaiah is being confronted with a proper vision of life. When our vision of what life is about is all too common and understood, God seeks to wake us up and bring clarity into our lives. Here, God's man, living among those in God's chosen nation, is confronted with the reality that he and his fellow countrymen just don't measure up. Their standards for living are well below what God intends. The measuring stick for relationships, true religion, and devotion to God has been cut short.

What Isaiah's episode teaches us is far reaching but simple. Building a life worth something begins and ends with God's standard for life. We cannot define our lives by measuring our activities, values, and actions against those of society at large. Our standard of measurement for decent living does not come from the opinions of our friends and coworkers. A strong future is not built by looking all around us for direction. We are unclean, and we, indeed, live among a nation of unclean people. When adultery is embraced by a culture and promoted through entertainment venues as normal, we suffer the consequences by way of divorce, emotionally crushed children, addictions, violence, and many other ills. Far from considering it normal, God suggests that adultery and all forms of sexual immorality are the very routes leading to ruin.

Rather than making light of these ills, joking about them, and encouraging others to pursue them if they "feel right," God tells us that if we pursue them we will find destruction. With every breech of God's commands, we find a corresponding consequence. Excessive drinking leads to addiction, relational breakdown, physical abuse, laziness, physical and psychological illness, and rising healthcare costs. Lying, cheating, and stealing lead to emotional, financial, and physical incarceration. Racism begets hatred, and hatred begets violence, suppression, and societal breakdown. The rewards of following the masses are less than appealing once seen for what they are. Building a life worth living requires moving beyond the majority view. Wide is the road to destruction, we are told; the narrow road is the preferable choice (Matt. 7:13-14 NIV).

God confronts Isaiah and the nation's viewpoint head on. The message is heard loud and clear by Isaiah, who literally falls on his face before God. The vision of who God is totally transforms him. The lesson here is one we all need to remember. Only in seeing God for who He is do we really view ourselves as we really are. When we take our eyes off the prevailing cultural view of normal and focus on God, then, and only then, can life come into focus. Until that happens, we live in spiritual blindness. When making decisions about life, we have got to come to a place where we measure those choices on what God has to say about the outcome. When tempted to jump the fence and look for greener grass, we need to remember that God warns us that the grass, though different, may not be greener.

What those who make that leap over the fence always find is crabgrass, ant hills, and a lawn that still needs mowing. Moreover, what God assures us of is that those who choose to go beyond the boundaries He provides lose the protection, safety, and blessing of being in His good plan. When tempted as a nation to embrace laws and legislation that deteriorate our society, we risk the fate of Rome and other civilizations that have come and gone.

In our distorted view of our national moral superiority, we have become blinded to our need of God's goodness in our midst. Our view of good is so far removed from God's goodness. This reality came like a soul tsunami to Isaiah as he realized how far off he and his nation were from the mark set by God. Isaiah, the best of examples, and the chosen nation had drifted too far from the shoreline of God's principles. The potential for destruction in those uncharted waters is great.

Isaiah's vision is instructive for another reason. A vision of the astounding radiance of God's goodness exposes the reality of every human heart. Even our best intentions are stained with the spot of sin. The philosophy of many moral commentators in the media and print today would suggest that we are all ultimately "good." This holy man would tell us a different story. Rather than viewing the human heart as "good," Isaiah sees his heart for what it really is—full of sin and short of the moral mark (Rom. 3:23 NIV).

Only when we see God for who He is can we truly understand who we are in light of that reality. An accurate view of the character of God is what tempers the proud heart and the proud nation. A glimpse of the splendor of God is enough to make even the best among us run for cover. Isaiah's reaction to his view of this Supreme Being left him "undone." The spiritual leader, rather than thinking he had a right to be there, lost his composure. He literally fell on His face in a state of panic over this new view of himself in light of God's perfect purity. I ask again, could it be that God has allowed or even sent certain national disasters to call our view of life into question? Have we become too self-assured?

The vision does not stop with God's assaulting our view of life, and here is the beauty of the Holy One. In the moment that Isaiah owns up to his own moral desolation in the sight of God, the hand of heaven reaches down to him, offers forgiveness and cleansing, and even ushers him into service! In spite of his lack of ability to live up to the standard of heaven, heaven itself extends an invitation to this one in need of grace—an invitation to serve as a spokesman no less!

This is the message of the Gospel. In seeing God for who He is, and in viewing life as it should be viewed, we see ourselves for what we are, we come undone. We submit ourselves to God, and He picks us up, dusts us off, and ushers us into His service in order that we might tell others of this great grace. He humbles us and then provides the very means for rebuilding our lives and the lives of others. He is capable of doing this not only with individual souls but also with cities, nations, and the world. There is truly hope for building a better future. God challenges our view of reality in order that He may build us up. When life is turned upside down and our routine altered in dramatic fashion, God is in the mix.

Wherever we have been, whatever we have done, God, the Standard, stands ready and waiting for us to acknowledge our lack of virtue and our need of Him. The soul that is willing to see God for who He is will gain a glimpse not only of the holiness of God, but also of His amazing grace. As we give God room to show Himself to us, He is able to build enduring structures of grace in our lives. Oh, that we might taste and see that the Lord is good (Ps. 34:8 NIV). He is truly good.

He is able to give more than enough grace to cover all our sins (Rom. 5:20). He is able to give us joy in excess of all our pain. He is capable of extending to us a hope and a future despite the devastation all around. He is the only one who can expose the reality of our impure heart while offering a full soul-makeover. He can and will do it if we give Him a chance. He will bring us to the floor when our vision is distorted. He will not allow us to continue living life apart from Him without having to endure the consequences.

We must turn around, move in a different direction, and look to His agenda if we are to find a life worth living. In that process of being brought low, our view is corrected, things become clear again, and He gives us His grace to pick up and build again. As was the case for the woman caught in adultery, He points out the destruction that should be self-evident, and then He picks up the pieces, rebuilds our souls, and calls us to dreams in line with His standards. We must open our eyes. We must get a glimpse of Him if we are to rebuild the right way.

A New Outlook: ·
A Storm Hero Finds Purpose

Kirk McNight, as it turns out, is a storm hero. Caught in the middle of the fury brought on by Katrina, he had his worldview changed dramatically. Growing up in New Orleans, this African-American kid lived life the hard way. The streets of the Big Easy had molded Kirk in ways that left him with little hope for a bright future. Out of school, without a model family, and living life by the moment, Kirk was headed for disaster.

I had the privilege of meeting him when he was brought to church by an entire family of unsung heroes. The Bradfords have been involved with meeting the needs of the underprivileged and the street-hardened teens of the Greater New Orleans area for some time. They have regularly opened their arms and hearts to those whom most of us consider to be lost causes. It is not uncommon for them to meet people on the street for the first time, have them in church the next day, and set them on a course of discipleship. Kirk McNight was one of those teens the Bradfords happened upon at a critical time in his life.

A tall, good-looking kid, and a decent basketball player, Kirk is a natural leader. Leadership, as we all know, can be used for good or ill. Prior to Katrina, Kirk's leadership was not put to positive use, but when Katrina came through the city and left many underprivileged citizens without resources or help, things began to change for Kirk. Finding himself surrounded by desperate conditions, Kirk could have wound up like those around him, looting and taking any measure to fend for self.

As it turned out, however, Kirk spent days fighting for the needs of others in the stagnant floodwaters of New Orleans. For several days, he waded through chest-deep filth to find food and water for the elderly, the ill, and those trapped by the rising waters. Rather than abandoning those around him and getting himself to higher ground, Kirk McNight devoted his time in the days following the storm to the better good. Though everything in his past had taught him to take care of himself, Kirk found a new awakening, a new view.

As he tells it, that new view began with the influence of the Bradfords telling him about the hope and future that God could provide. In Kirk's last conversation with Angie Bradford, he heard about God's good plans for him. That conversation continually came to mind as Kirk fought his way through the devastation day after day. As he waded through the stench, Kirk would remember being told that he was a natural leader and that God could use his leadership for good if he would allow Him to do so. Kirk was told that God would cause his entire life to fall apart if need be in order to bring him to Himself.

Shortly after Kirk's talk with Angie, his world began to unravel. His relationships with family were increasingly strained, and he was eventually kicked out of his home. Separated from loved ones, and feeling alone, Kirk easily could have turned toward selfish pursuits during this horrible calamity. In the end, he chose to look at life differently and recognize God's call to embrace a new way of living. As Kirk recently told the Bradfords, "Everything that you said came true. I got into a fight with my stepdad, and he kicked me out. I had to move to New Orleans with my aunt. Things were going wrong there, and then the storm hit. I went to church this morning, and everything the pastor said was something that you've said to me. I just want you to know that I'm going to go to church every Sunday, and I'm going to do something with my life."

Kirk has now become an example to many and a storm hero in Texas, where many ask him for his autograph. In the midst of a historic storm, God got his attention, changed his view, and transformed his life. He is now making an effort to build a new life God's way. He is working on his GED, going to church, and searching for his next mission. God has a way of taking us through the storms, carrying us away to bigger things, and bringing good all around us as He unfolds His plans. Seen with eyes of faith, the future looks bright. Sometimes, the path to greater things begins with a storm.

A Bigger View: Parrots, Savants, and Concentration Camps

Amidst the rubble and the kind of devastation we see on television everyday, it is easy to have our view of life reduced to something less than we would hope for. Those too familiar with tragedy and grief oftentimes lose passion for life and give up on dreams. Driving through the Lakeview area of New Orleans recently, one of the sections of town drowned by Katrina, I had an eye-opening experience. Everywhere I drove, as far as I could see, there was nothing but gray rubble. Every house had a water line nearly up to the roof, every yard was covered with stacks of molded and ruined furniture, every street was littered with mud-caked cars and trucks, and cast-off refrigerators lined the streets.

After driving through the area where I once lived, I began to have respiratory problems and headaches. Just one hour spent in what once was a thriving, beautiful part of town left me sad and depressed. How can anyone view life with optimism amidst this kind of drastic situation, I thought. After I rode through Lakeview to get a sense of the challenges lying ahead for so many, I drove out to the lakefront area where the Yacht Club used to be. It was a staggering sight. On the property that was once a playground for the city's rich there was nothing but piles of useless and damaged "toys."

Every yacht and sailboat that was there prior to the hurricane is now part of a large pile of debris. Boats are smashed upon one another, yachts are strewn everywhere, and the once brightly colored sails that made the area picturesque are gone or shredded. As I walked through the maze of broken dreams, I came upon one large sailboat, ironically named "Stuff." How quickly our stuff can be gone.

Making my way from the lakefront I came upon a very large

puddle of standing water and had to slow down. As I was slowing, I noticed what at first appeared to be a bunch of dirty birds playing in the water. They looked like everything else in the area, battered and gray. But as I got closer I noticed a marvelous thing. Amidst the calamity, mess, and misery, playing in the water in the bright sunshine was a flock of parrots! It was the first color I had seen all morning. Bright greens, yellows, and oranges were splashing in the water and enjoying the day.

The juxtaposition of these amazing creatures in that setting was profound. My senses came alive, and I had a thought. No matter how bleak it looks around us, regardless of storms endured, there are still signs of life, beauty, and hope. Then I was reminded of God's care for even the birds of the earth, and the scriptures promise that He cares even more for us as humans (Luke 12:24), the crown of His creation (Ps. 8:5). Even in the worst of circumstances there are glimpses of the divine at work.

Often, I have taken educational detours to branch out into new fields for a period of time. Brain research is one area into which I detoured for a short period while in graduate school. Understanding how the mind works and the phenomenal complexities with which God has created us is fascinating. At times we have all heard about the different hemispheres of the brain, the left brain/right brain functionality, and the various theories regarding why one person is a math whiz and another more philosophical. It is intriguing stuff.

Recently, I viewed a program on television that utterly captivated me. It was a look into the world of a unique and very small population of people who are both severely mentally impaired and extraordinarily musically gifted. These savants, and the implications for study in the field of brain research, are astonishing.

One of the young men featured on the program, Rex, is blind and mentally retarded, yet astoundingly gifted musically. Talking with Rex is very difficult, and his mind is seemingly hampered in every way. But at the piano, the whole world changes for this young man. Rex is a musical genius. Listening to him play, while looking at him, with his mental and physical challenges very apparent, one cannot help but be joyfully confused.

How is it that someone so "messed up," by most people's assumptions, can at the same time be so brilliant? Listening to him play and recognizing that something marvelous is going on inside his brain convinces me that those who would support the right to abort such a "problem" have missed out on the glorious mysteries of God's creation. The suggestion that physical and mental disaster discovered in the womb prior to birth should allow for the termination of life has, perhaps, robbed the world of many amazing gifts and contributions to society. Likewise, the termination of a passion for life amidst the disabilities that life brings our way robs us of the potential brilliance that lies ahead. We must learn to look for the divine spark, that flicker of beauty that still radiates in the darkness around us.

Our definition of life is inadequate when we view it from a human perspective. Moreover, our assumptions as to "quality of life" are far too narrow. I wonder if, in reality, Rex and those like him know the splendid graces of our Creator more than we who are "normal." Do such people have access to the operation of faculties more in tune with what God created us for despite the obvious hindrances we see in them? It is a question worth pondering. Is life worth living even when it looks terribly messed up? Should we joyfully fight rather than give in to depression, anxiety, and bitterness? The answers are obvious I think.

Another of the savants featured on the program was referred to as the "human iPod." Derek is a living testimony of the dignity that coexists with disaster. More severely mentally disabled than Rex, Derek is also a musical genius. At the piano, his mind works magic. To the onlooker, it would seem that the entire world is closed off to him. In reality, a world more spectacular than most any of us have ever envisioned lives within him. Derek can not only play the piano, he can play any song he has ever heard in his entire life note for note!

The great compositions of the classical masters can be played without a moment of preparation, and splendidly. Derek can not only recall the classical masters, he can also play anything from any era or genre up to today. More than that, he can be asked to play a contemporary rock song as if a classical master had composed it and pull it off! The divine spark, the grand design, the bigger view is apparent when we sit in awe before such amazing people.

Our view is so small, our passion so easily quenched, our hope so easily dashed. Though the magnitude of pain, destruction, and disability piles up around us every day, in the midst of it all, the parrots are still at play, the genius is still at work, and the hand of the divine One is still involved. Savants like Derek and Rex remind us that as complex and, at times, as indiscernible as life can be, God is at work. He has worlds awaiting us we have never even dreamed of.

If New Orleans is to have a real hope for rebuilding, and if anyone is to find energy for building a life despite overwhelming obstacles, a glimpse of the divine must come into view. A bigger view of life as we know it is our only hope in finding passion to press ahead.

Corrie ten Boom, whose story has been told all across the globe, found a glimpse of God even amidst the horror of the Nazi concentration camps. Captured and sent to slave in the death camps for housing Jews during the Holocaust, Corrie found God despite the pain and suffering around her. Seeing members of her own family dying at the hands of these cruel forces did not keep her from finding the will to continue pursuing a better way.

Eventually, after enduring much hardship and fighting the good fight of faith, Corrie ten Boom made it out and went on to tell the world of the horrors imposed by the Nazis. More important, she was able to tell the world of the hope to be found in God no matter the depth of despair. The essence of Corrie's testimony has been her view of a big God. Her view of a God that is bigger than the challenges of this life gave her strength from day to day when others around her had turned to hatred, bitterness, and deep sadness. Her big view of God eventually brought her out of the camps, miraculously kept her from death, and gloriously led her on to tour the world telling thousands of the power, passion, and hope found in Christ.

Corrie ten Boom, like those parrots at play in the puddles of destruction, was the light of God during one of the darkest moments in world history. Every dark night of the soul can be illuminated by the light of God if we will remove the dark glasses with which we are accustomed to seeing life and exchange our viewpoint for a much larger one. The view from above sees past the loss and the obstacles and keeps the end goal in sight. As big as the mess may appear, down the road is a better place. We must learn to fight our way through the destruction to that destination.

One Good Cup of Coffee Can Change Everything: The Story of Starbucks

I am a coffee fanatic. For me, a great day consists of a good book, time to write, jazz playing in the background, and a great cup of Starbucks. Life just does not get much better than that. Often, that book I might be reading while sipping on a latte would be a biographical account of someone who has overcome odds in life to accomplish something significant. Howard Schultz is one of those people. His story is about seeing life beyond present surroundings.

Schultz, the CEO of Starbucks, was not always on top of the world. Looking at him now one might be tempted to think his life has always been easy. This megarich corporate hero, basketball team owner, and head of a company that has become part of our culture did not always live the good life. In fact, if you read his book, *Pour Your Heart into It,* you will find that his early days growing up in Brooklyn were full of challenges.

Schultz cut his teeth in a blue-collar home watching his father struggle to make it all work. Taking in all the challenges of his setting as a young person laid the groundwork for his future. Rather than perceiving the struggles as too much to overcome, Howard set his mind to forging a better future. After watching his father labor to put bread on the table and after witnessing the impact of his father's broken ankle upon the family's ability to survive, Howard began to set his sights beyond Brooklyn. He would have to chart new waters, as no one in his family had even gone to college, let alone hit it big.

Eventually, Howard Schultz graduated from college and landed a good job, one that most people at that time would have held onto for life. Far from the Bayview projects in which he grew up, Schultz landed a well-paying position with Xerox and was given the best sales training available. Just a few years into his well-respected job, however, Howard was growing restless and looking for something that offered a greater challenge.

Then came the opportunity to join a housewares company, where Schultz was able to get in on the ground floor. He was sent off to Sweden for some time of training, and there he absorbed the European culture and developed the European zest for life. As he tells it, he was overwhelmed. While working for this company, Schultz was transferred to a division where he was forced to sell products in which he had no interest.

Feeling out of place and frustrated, he threatened to quit. The company, realizing they would be losing a vital asset in Schultz, actually moved him back to the housewares division, promoted him to vice-president, and increased his pay. He was given responsibility for an entire division of the company, a hefty salary, a company car, an expense account, and unlimited travel, which took him to Sweden a number of times a year.

While working in this capacity, Schultz's passion to see beyond the present was piqued once again. Having oversight of a division that was selling kitchen equipment and housewares, Schultz was intrigued by the reports that showed a small coffee company placing unusually large orders for coffeemakers. Motivated to check on this Seattle-based company, Howard Schultz went up to visit and find out what was happening with this four-store retailer.

As Schultz tells it in his book, he was enamored with the setting in Seattle when he got off the plane, and then hooked on the coffee after his first few sips. More than just good coffee, it was an atmosphere, an experience, a new way of viewing time spent around a cup of java. Wanting to know more about the business and the passion for coffee that was evident, Schultz sat down with the owners to hear the story of how they began with a meager investment of less than $15,000, during a time when opening a coffee shop in Seattle made no sense at all.

Seattle was on its way down after a major recession. The theme of the day was found on billboards that read, "Would the last person leaving Seattle turn the lights out?" All the studies, all the odds, all the current information suggested that a coffee company was not the way to go. The founders, however, were passionate about the dream, loved what they were doing, and were willing to look beyond the present surrounding to a hope-filled future.

As time went on, and as Howard Schultz got to know the owners better, he became more and more intrigued by the whole thing. Along the way, his trips to Europe had won him over to a joy and pursuit of life that the American culture lacked. Eventually, it became his dream to bring a taste of that life to America through, of all things, coffee. Willing to put aside all the success he had attained and the secure life he and his family had been enjoying, Schultz asked the owners if he could become a part of the company. Friends and family told him he was crazy. Convinced he could play a part in expanding the Starbucks vision, Schultz took a leap forward and asked if he could join the ranks.

After a long dinner meeting, and a night filled with Schultz sharing his vision for an expanded Starbucks, the owners and their backers told him no. Howard was crushed, but still determined to make his way in. He went to the owners again, gave his heart-filled and impassioned hard sell, and eventually convinced them to take him on. As Schultz describes it in his book, "A whole new world had just opened up in front of my eyes, like a scene in *The Wizard of Oz* when everything changes from black and white to color. This barely imaginable dream was really going to happen."

It seemed like everything was coming into focus for Howard Schultz, and his new dream was unfolding. Just as he and the family were preparing to leave, however, he received a call from his mother telling him that his father was diagnosed with lung cancer and given only a year to live. Now what? he thought. Torn between pursuing his dream and staying with his father in what would be, perhaps, his last days, Schultz had to make a huge decision. After wrestling with the enormity of this soul storm and being encouraged by his father to pursue his new life, Schultz and his family set out for Seattle.

That challenge, like many others to come, would test Schultz's resolve and commitment to pursue a better future. There were, of course, many more challenges, obstacles, and pitfalls along the way. As history records it now, however, Howard Schultz's decision to set off for a bigger dream, his ability to see beyond the present, his wider view, led to the development of a staggering string of successes. After many more big decisions and some hefty risk-taking, Schultz eventually came to a place of majority ownership interest in Starbucks. The company and its coffee are now engrained in our culture, and the rate of growth and profitability have been the stuff of which dreams are made. There really is nothing like a good cup of coffee!

So what's the point? Starbucks is an example of what can take place in the soul of an individual, a city, or a nation when a view toward a better future is embraced and pursued with passion. The present surroundings do not have to be the end of the story. What we are experiencing now does not have to determine who we are and what we become. Belief in a better way, the willingness to look beyond the here and now, and the courage to take risks can produce the life we have always dreamed of.

God has never quit on His dream to call us unto Himself, and He has always specialized in using less-than-perfect surroundings to get us right where He wants us. He desires that we taste and see that He is good, and He is able to make our lives a pleasing aroma before Him. The lives of men like Joseph, Job, David, and many others attest to this reality. The lives of many displaced by Katrina will, in the end, become testimonies not of personal displacement but of divine placement for a better day, a bigger view, a dream fulfilled. It can happen. It is happening.

Divine Displacement

Eleanor Roosevelt once said, "Do one thing every day that scares you." The story of Starbucks is a testimony to the results of taking risks and moving on from present surroundings, whether comfortable or uncomfortable, and moving toward something scary but good. It is not always easy, however, to take that leap. At times, God brings us to a place where the moment is ripe, and we must act or miss it. Because He does not reveal the grand scheme and the end goal to us, we often pull back in fear and decide to stay put and settle for "normal."

It is God's goal for us to recognize, by faith, that He is working for our good and that He desires to bring miraculous turning points into our lives. These "watershed" moments can redefine our lives and our futures, and can even save our lives at times. Gary Keife, a resident of the Greater New Orleans area who was displaced by Katrina, has come to see this reality up close. His story is told by writer Jan LeBlanc in the Hurricane Katrina Special Edition of *Inside Northside* magazine.

In the months prior to Katrina, Gary had been facing a life-and-death battle against the clock. Awaiting a liver transplant and without a donor in sight, Gary's condition was becoming increasingly worse, and he was losing hope. His body was beginning to break down, and despite good medical care in New Orleans, no donor could be found. With his body failing and his hopes diminishing, Gary was losing the battle against time and finding it hard to care for his son. The cruel reality was that every day of his life he would wait by the phone for the call that would tell him the donor had finally been found. That call just never came. As a result, Gary's future was looking less than desirable.

The last thing Gary needed, at least in his mind, was a hurricane.

Fearful to move out of harm's way, and hoping the hurricane would come and go, Gary decided to ride out the storm in his home just north of New Orleans. Displacement, he thought, would mean even bigger problems in his battle to get a liver transplant. An evacuation was out of the question. Katrina had a different plan. Surviving the storm in his home as trees were being snapped like toothpicks and thrown everywhere, Gary was facing a real problem. It became apparent very soon after the storm that staying put was not an option. Trees had fallen on his house, electricity was gone, roads were blocked, phone lines were severed, and the city was shut down. Gary realized he needed to get out of town no matter how risky that undertaking seemed in light of his condition.

Though displacement at this moment in his life did not seem like the road to hope, Gary set out to northern Louisiana to stay with a friend. After receiving a phone call from Gary asking for a place to stay, his friend contacted a local hospital in Shreveport to set up a visit so that proper care could be administered. The doctors, shocked by Gary's physical state and the severity of his illness, immediately bumped him to the top of the donor list.

In less than two weeks, a donor surfaced, and Gary was scheduled for a transplant. The surgery was successful, and Gary was on his way back to health. What seemed to be the end of all hope had become the road to an unexpected miracle. The displacement, in the end, became a divine appointment. As Gary put it, "Everything was truly a miracle. . . . When the hurricane forced us away, we thought there was no hope. But if not for the evacuation, I would still be there waiting."

The images on CNN and the headlines in all of the papers tell of tens of thousands of lives that have been uprooted. Families have been broken up, and immediate, convulsive change has forced many to reconsider where life is taking them. The question of where to rebuild and how to rebuild is an everyday reality for so many. Gary's story and many others demonstrate that hope still exists. When we are tempted to question what good can come of such circumstances, we must recognize that unexpected miracles may be on the way.

For some, rebuilding will mean a return to the city. For others, the future will unfold in another place. As was true for Gary Keife and Howard Schultz, sometimes our greatest chance for a life beyond normal lies far away from what we have always seen and known. Though that may seem scary at times, we must be willing to take a chance and venture out. When the waters all around us appear to be so tumultuous that our end seems certain, we must walk on those waters just as Peter did. In doing so, we may very well find a greater future unfolding for us. God is at work in these watershed events.

The Call to Something More:
Walking on Water

What if you could walk on water? Pursuing the "what if" is not easy, but the rewards are worth everything that is risked. We often refer to this hypothetical dream as if it has never happened, or we refer to it as if only one person has ever done it. In reality, Jesus was not the only person to have ever done this. Earlier in the book, we looked at the first part of the account, but now let's look at Matthew's version of the rest of the story:

> And in the fourth watch of the night he came to them, walking on the sea. But when the disciples saw him walking on the sea, they were terrified, and said, "It is a ghost!" and they cried out in fear. But immediately Jesus spoke to them, saying, "Take heart; it is I. Do not be afraid."
> And Peter answered him, "Lord, if it is you, command me to come to you on the water." He said, "Come." So Peter got out of the boat and walked on the water and came to Jesus. (Matt. 14:25-29)

What an experience this must have been. Amidst a major storm, with the winds howling, and in all likelihood surrounded by waves as tall as Peter stood himself, this man got up nerve enough to take an enormous risk. He got out of the boat, and walked on water! What an absurd notion for anyone in the real world to even suggest something so stupid. Who did this guy think he was anyway? And if it were not ridiculous enough already to attempt something so bizarre, this guy wanted to try this in the middle of a violent storm. What arrogance!

But was Peter really arrogant, stupid, and overconfident, or was he pursuing life as God intended it to be pursued? We get too few big moments in life. What if Howard Schultz had taken no for an answer when he was first refused in his petitions to join the ranks of Starbucks? What if Gary Keife had never left his home and traveled away from the surroundings that had kept a liver transplant from taking place? What if the man crippled with palsy had never been carried to Jesus for healing? What happens if we miss the big moments life brings our way and fail to venture out in new directions? Do we settle for less? We certainly do.

Those who have never taken a risk on faith in God are missing the abundant life He offers. The fear of giving up what we know can leave us spiritually crippled in this life, never knowing what it means to live a life of significance. Get out of the boat; take a chance on God. See what He is capable of doing in and with your life. God can and will instill new visions, bigger dreams, and greater clarity in your life when you trust Him for your purposes.

He may call you to things you never imagined, or He may fulfill that desire in you that has never yet been voiced, planned, or attempted. He may use you in leadership to help others rebuild homes, cities, countries, and lives. He may use you to bring a plan into shape that will help numerous people recapture their lives. Are you willing to take a risk? Are you willing to step out of the boat and onto the water?

Peter's venture toward a massive, God-sized risk was not perfectly executed, but it certainly was filled with drama, excitement, and an exhilarating experience of the power of God. The story continues to unfold as we read:

> But when he saw the wind, he was afraid, and beginning to sink he cried out, "Lord, save me." Jesus immediately reached out his hand and took hold of him, saying to him, "O you of little faith, why did you doubt?" And when he got into the boat, the wind ceased. And those in the boat worshiped him, saying, "Truly you are the Son of God." (Matt. 14:30-33)

Peter, a man taking an audacious risk, started out in confidence and strength, and then got distracted by the storm around him, causing him to lose focus and lose sight of his dream to do what had never been done before. In the midst of the storms of our lives, God is calling us to get out of the boat and take a chance on something more. He always wants to pull us beyond ourselves toward bigger things. When we are willing to take a risk on His agenda, the unthinkable dream can come into shape. When our eyes focus too much on life from our viewpoint, however, we settle for less, and we begin to sink. We must learn to ask, amidst the winds and waves, what God is calling us to do.

As it was for Peter, so it will be with us, there will be moments of fear and distraction. We will not get it right all of the time. Storms will continue to rage around us, and we will feel vulnerable. Thankfully, the Creator looks on us with compassion and love, and extends His reach to us during those moments. God does not take joy in our drowning. Rather, He desires that we walk on the water beside Him with poise, composure, and strength, no matter how big the waves that threaten us.

What is God calling you to now? Whether you find yourself at this moment amidst great trouble or on top of the world, God's call is the same. It rains on the just and the unjust, and it is also true that the just and the unjust find success. In either place, God is calling us to know, love, and serve Him. The void that exists for those who have gotten more than a life's share of rain is the same void that exists in the hearts of those who have seen a life of plenty. The call to take a risk on knowing God remains. The call to risk our life in order to know and follow the Lord is the decision by which we will all be measured.

As Saint Augustine suggested long ago, there exists a void in all of us, a God-ordained void that cannot and will not be filled with anything other than Him. We will find no rest until we find our rest in Him. Building a life God's way entails a release of all that makes us secure and an embrace of a future lived under the gaze of the One who controls the winds and the waves. What if you took that chance? What would your life be like if you stepped out onto those waters? There's only one way to find out. Don't leave that risk untried.

Extreme Makeover: Catastrophe Edition

"The Next Big One," the feature article in the September 19, 2005, edition of *Business Week* magazine, is one that cannot be ignored. Katrina, as we are all aware, has brought an intense focus on America's state of preparation for disasters of all kinds. What was witnessed by people across the globe in the wake of Katrina was a reality that few of us ever expected to see. America, it seems, is ill-prepared to care for its own amidst a major catastrophe.

As Bruce Nussbaum points out in his *Business Week* article, national officials are beginning to admit to America's need for a more secure disaster plan. Disaster is a reality of life, and our state of preparedness must meet the challenges that we know are ahead of us. Quoting an expert on the preparedness issue, Dr. Irwin E. Redlener, Nussbaum records his comments: "The country really just is not prepared for a major catastrophic event. . . . Whatever it is—the Big One in San Francisco, a terrorist attack—it doesn't matter. . . ." Just as we were unable to contemplate the idea of planes becoming bombs and flying through our trophies of accomplishment, we still appear unable to soberly acknowledge our vulnerability to the ravages of nature. The geographic, emotional, physical, and spiritual landscape of the entire Gulf Coast region has been dramatically altered by Katrina. One thing is sure: It will not be the same. On September 11, 2001, the physical, emotional, and spiritual landscape of our nation was impacted by the terrorist attacks. In many ways, we have not been the same since. How many of us can watch a plane fly over a skyscraper and not wonder if it is happening again? Yet in too many ways, we are the same.

Though the impact of 9-11 was immediate, dramatic, and far-reaching, years later we still wrestle with our hunger for the now, our thirst for pleasure, our lack of a moral compass, and our apathy regarding important social issues. As severely as these national disasters have affected us, it appears we are still in need of a major soul makeover. When will we realize, in light of the calamities that come our way, that we must prepare our lives, homes, cities, and country for these storms?

Our lack of ability to prepare is an indication of our "readiness" for life. Perhaps we do not prepare for the storms of life because the reality is too stark to ponder, and so we put it off until it happens. Or, perhaps, we fail to prepare adequately because we are too consumed with living for the moment and too busy entertaining ourselves to consider the depressing possibilities that lie ahead. Maybe we think that when the time comes, we can just throw a bunch of money at the problem, and that will fix it.

What 9-11, Katrina, Oklahoma City, and other disasters have shown us, however, is that we must consider life with a bigger view in mind. We must live life to the fullest and enjoy our short time here, but we must view our days in light of eternity. There will be good days, and there will be bad days. We must prepare for both. The blessings of life are many, and we ought to take them in — good food, a great cup of coffee, majestic music, the arts, mountains, beaches, volcanoes, rain forests, and wonders too vast to list. But we must recognize that these wonders are not all there is to life. We cannot expect to withstand the brutal forces of life's storms if we do not recognize that life is much more than pleasure on every hand.

Just as we must, as a country, prepare ahead of time for the disasters ahead, we must also prepare our hearts, minds, and souls for the onslaught of life's tougher realities. The ability to withstand the storms of terminal illness, hatred, betrayal, injustice, financial setback, divorce, mental illness, spiritual hypocrisy, and displacement comes from an inner life that has made preparation prior to the storms. When we are not prepared, as we have seen, the devastation left behind is hard to imagine. It is becoming clear that America's disaster preparedness plan needs an extreme makeover.

Anne Rice, the famous author of a number of books, several of which have been made into movies, has recently announced her own makeover. A native of New Orleans, Rice admits that her past writing, which has gained her enormous fame, has been characterized by darkness. That has all changed, suggests Rice. She has had a soul makeover. Now, as she tells it, her mission, her calling, is to write fictional works that point to her return to and her understanding of Christ and the church.

The makeover in this case is nothing short of extreme. Recently, when asked by a news commentator how she would have responded to her publishers had they refused to work with this mission to write about Christ, Rice said, "I have no choice. I have to do this. I would have just found another publisher, though my present publisher is like my family. I have come home. I have come back to the church." That's a makeover. It will take a makeover of extreme fashion to remake our American culture, which has drifted far from its roots and its Judeo-Christian values. Likewise, it takes an extreme makeover to transform our souls.

In New Orleans and the Gulf Coast region, an extreme makeover is needed now more than ever. As a result of a lack of preparedness, New Orleans has been reduced to a city full of rubble and toxic mold. Now that the picture is becoming clearer, it appears that inadequately constructed levees were responsible for a good bit of the flooding. Tens of thousands of residents lost homes, lives, possessions, and dreams because the preparedness plans and protection systems never received the long overdue makeover that had been talked about.

Had the levees held, it is likely that New Orleans would be in far better physical shape today. Had buses been available, many of the thousands left stranded would have made it out of the city, and much of the madness could have been prevented. Had a better escape plan been designed to help the elderly and infirm, far fewer would have died in nursing facilities and in the attics of flooded homes. Had New Orleans been better prepared for the realities of life, this jewel of a city could have withstood the test with more grace. Had city, state, and federal agencies gotten their game plan together and implemented a coherent and effective strategy for disaster recovery, New Orleans' impact from the forces of nature would have been dramatically minimized.

What is true for New Orleans in this regard is also true of us individually. Without a proper strategy for dealing with the storms of life, we are in extreme danger. When we fail to look at all of life's potentialities and the long-term impact of our decisions, we set the stage for a dramatic crash. When men and women do not develop their inner lives in a way that prepares them for the challenges of marriage, people get hurt and lives are turned upside down. When a teenager decides to give in to the moment and takes his eyes off of the future, certain consequences necessarily follow.

Our plans and the execution of those plans for life preparedness determine how life will unfold for us. The integrity of our protection system is the critical factor when the floods come our way. Unless a moral levee, constructed with strength and precision, surrounds our heart, the temptations of life will always have too strong a pull for us.

If our life is to have staying power, grace, joy, and fulfillment, it must be properly prepared and well constructed. If not, as we have seen, and as Bruce Nussbaum has pointed out, the ramifications of catastrophe could be too much to bear. In his article, Nussbaum points to potential disasters that lie ahead and the impact upon America and the world. His words should startle us and compel us to prepare for what is coming at some point in the future. His words point to the absolutely critical need to plan ahead and the desperate need we all have to construct a preparedness strategy that can protect against the coming scenarios that would spell our ruin.

In conjunction with Bruce Nussbaum's cover story, Catherine

Arnst and other writers developed a hypothetical scenario around the potential avian flu pandemic in order to demonstrate the implications for America and the global community. In this scenario, one in which the avian flu strikes Chicago, it is apparent that in a relatively short period of time, the spread of the deadly disease would dramatically change lives around the globe.

As many as 50 percent of those attacked by the disease die, with half between the ages of eighteen and forty. With the disease spreading around the globe, the United States would be unable to get assistance from other nations. The pandemic, compared to the Spanish flu pandemic of 1918-19, could kill up to 67 million Americans, a full 25 percent of the population. In Nussbaum's *Business Week* article, Michael T. Osterholm, an infectious disease expert at the University of Minnesota, suggests, "The difference between this and a hurricane is that all 50 states will be affected at the same time. And this crisis will last a year or more. It will utterly change the world."

In a chilling summary of the implications of this potential outbreak, the journalists studying the issue write the following, "The change would spread far beyond the number of deaths. Most experts predict that an avian flu outbreak in the U.S. would overwhelm hospitals, decimate workforces, and throw transportation and supply chains into chaos." The studies being conducted at this very moment are truly shocking. In a short period of time medical supplies and critical disaster response inventories would vanish, and the pressure upon global financial systems could quickly reach beyond the $150 billion mark.

As if that were not scary enough, the reality is potentially direr in light of the lack of a preparedness plan. The article continues, "Right now, the U.S. has no national pandemic preparedness plan, either for treating large numbers of patients or for dealing with the resulting economic and social disruptions. 'We can't handle a pandemic flu,' asserts Dr. [Edwin E.] Redlener of the National Center for Disaster Preparedness."

Just as the flu pandemic threatens life on our planet, so too we face growing soul pandemics in our lives. The spread of materialism, thirst for power, selfishness, racism, social injustice, poverty, greed, lust, alcoholism, disdain for absolute truth, and so many more diseases of the soul threaten to plunge our society into deeper moral decay. Without a well-thought-out plan for protecting our hearts and minds from those diseases, we can find ourselves in a critical state of need. Just as the spread of looting plunged the city of New Orleans into chaos, fear, and despair, so also does the looting of our souls bring destruction to all of those around us. As the spread of the avian flu threatens to reach tens of millions in our country alone, so does the growing cultural malaise threaten to wipe out the fabric of society.

If we are to have any hope of protecting our own lives from emptiness, and even destruction, we must construct a life that can withstand the temptations around us. If we are to build a life worth living, we need a plan that has stood the test of time. If we are going to find meaning and virtue in this life, and if we are going to have any hope of leaving a legacy, we must aim to build upon principles that can serve as a foundation for the soul. We must have a plan for funding the rebuilding of our souls. In the pages that follow I offer such a plan.

PART FIVE

A PREPAREDNESS PLAN FOR THE SOUL

All men die. Not all men really live.

— Braveheart

A Life Worth Living

The funding aspect of the country's preparedness planning is particularly intriguing to me. I have spent the majority of the last decade working in the investment world as a tangible asset broker. It has been my job to teach investors how to find truly rare and valuable collectible assets that have the potential to provide for a secure investment future.

What successful brokers, advisors, and clients know is that success in investing comes as a result of good planning and wise asset allocation. That is to say, an investor must have a solid plan based upon strong principles, and he must allocate his funds strategically based upon his core principles. A mastery of the fundamentals in investment philosophy and a commitment to them goes a long way toward success. Most people get hurt when they deviate from the game plan, looking for that unlikely but alluring "big score."

One investment guru I have studied in order to gain some insight into allocating resources is Warren Buffet, the Oracle of Omaha. Buffet is the second wealthiest man on the planet and the most successful investor in history. He is the only investor in history to outperform Standard and Poor's 2:1 over a thirty-year period. His success has come from strict adherence to some fundamental principles. Over time, I have developed a model for successful investing based upon my research, a close study of Buffet's philosophies, and the work of others. I have used these principles time and time again when building a strategy for my clients, and they provide a great analogy for us in our discussion of developing a preparedness plan for life.

Ultimately, as is the case for our country, and for us as individuals, we must make intelligent decisions when determining how to "fund" our plans for life. The degree to which we live a fulfilling life will be determined by our investing philosophy. If we fail to prepare and allocate the necessary funding for life's potentialities, we open ourselves up to soul pandemics from which we may never recover. As has been seen in New Orleans, when we fail to allocate for the strengthening of our protection systems, the consequences are severe. Let's look at the plan for soul preparedness.

A Game Plan for Life

Not too long ago, I had the good fortune of brokering a deal that gained a good bit of press. After quite a bit of study, negotiation, and planning, I was able to secure for my client one of the most important rare coins in the world, the famed 1913 Liberty Head "V" Nickel. At the time, the $3 million we invested represented the largest single retail coin transaction in history. When we announced the coin's sale, the story broke around the world via television, Internet, and newspapers. The newswires all told of the unique set of historical realities that make this coin so valuable.

Shortly after the press conferences and newscasts were done, I was asked to appear for an interview on National Public Radio's *Weekend Edition* program to tell the story of this coin. In every venue where the story was told, the focus was on the coin's history, the intrigue behind its minting, its theft from the mint, the pedigree of its ownership, and all the tales that make the story so exciting. But the story that was so compelling for me was what I had learned in the process of brokering the deal. It was the highlight of my investment career, and the coin was front and center in all of the trade publications, but for me the real importance was found in the construction of the deal.

In the brokering of the deal, I was renewed in my conviction that planning, strategy, and a compelling foundation are essential for any accomplishment worth pursuing. The principles upon which the deal was constructed are more important to me than the coin itself, and they have served to help guide me in building a life worth living. My hope is that in evaluating these principles you too will find a valuable plan for preparing your life for the future God has for you. As the disaster in New Orleans and the Gulf Coast region has demonstrated, a good plan can make a great deal of difference prior to and in the aftermath of a storm. Moreover, oftentimes, lack of planning and preparation result in destruction that could have been avoided.

The diligence we put into preparing our souls will determine the kind of future ahead of us. That being so, it is imperative that we plan well, and build a strong foundation. Storms are ahead, and the extent of the damages will largely depend upon our readiness. If we are to build a life worth living, and if we are to construct a life that can endure hardship with grace and strength, we must hold to some sure principles. The principles I offer here, if embraced, can provide the building material needed to construct an inner life that will withstand the winds to come. Investing in these concepts will yield enormous returns in the future and will provide a kind of life that is all too rarely seen today. Here are the elements of a game plan for a life worth living:

(1) Quality over Quantity

Mr. Buffett would rather own a handful of quality companies than a huge portfolio with a slew of companies. Why? Because quality rather than quantity is what produces return. When I placed the 1913 "V" Nickel, it made headlines all over the world. What the headlines did not reveal is the hard work put into the strategy long before we got to that historic achievement.

Because we had previously selected our coin investments on their quality rather than quantity, we had the chance to "trade" a handful of world-class coins to get the coin of coins, the "V" Nickel. Any smart art investor will tell you that you are better off investing in one Picasso than in two hundred lesser-known works. Why? Return, return, return. So, if you want to live a life worth living, if you want a life prepared for the future, you must invest your heart, mind, soul, and entire being in those things that yield a quality life: integrity, truth, faithfulness, sobriety, devotion to family, love.

As we have noted, it is not true that he who has the most toys wins. Years ago while living in Chicago, I heard a sermon I remember to this day. John Ortberg preached a message titled, "It

All Goes Back in the Box." To get his point across regarding the spiritual and emotional bankruptcy in investing all of our passions and efforts in our jobs and our possessions, he used the game of Monopoly as a metaphor.

At the end of life, just like in the game of Monopoly, it all goes back in the box. When the game is over, all the houses, cars, money, and other trinkets must be left behind. If we spend our life chasing things, we will miss out on the quality of life offered to us by Jesus, who said He would give us life, and life abundantly (John 10:10). The psalmist writes in Psalm 27:4, "One thing I have asked of the LORD, that I will seek after: that I may dwell in the house of the LORD all the days of my life, to gaze upon the beauty of the LORD and to inquire in his temple" (ESV). The quality of that one thing beats all the rest the world has to offer. In order to have a life prepared for potential disasters ahead, we must pursue quality of life over quantity of things.

(2) Blue Chip Values

We must invest in those things that have historically produced returns over a long period of time. How has faithfulness outperformed adultery? How has truthfulness outperformed lying? How has self-sacrifice outperformed greed? How has giving outperformed taking? Those ideals that we all agree have compelling and life-giving force are the things we ought to pursue in this life. All the other stuff loses its appeal when reality sets in, and it always does at some point. Just read the headlines every day to see how unfulfilled all the Hollywood stars really are despite "having all the fun."

Sin may be fun for a season, but once the season is over, the pain sets in. The pain of disrupted families, lost opportunities, broken hearts, and diseased bodies is too much to endure. A moment of fun never prepares us for the future. Living for the moment leaves our levee weakened and unable to protect us in the event of rising waters. Momentary pleasures never provide the material needed to strengthen us for the winds of change blowing our way.

Any time we are making an attempt to build or rebuild a life, critical decisions must be made that affect those around us. If we are to make good decisions, ones that promote a strong and meaningful life, those decisions must be made with an eye toward community and a focus upon family. We were made for relationships with others. Selfish isolation does not promote the kind of life we were created for. If our plan to rebuild our lives contradicts or hinders God's plan for family and community, it ought to be questioned. Our first calling is, of course, to God and His goals for us, but we must recognize that His first objective for society is the establishment and building of the family unit.

The deterioration of American society and the breakdown in our communities is largely due to the abandonment of the family unit as our chief priority. I am grateful that, though I grew up in a broken home, my mother demonstrated a commitment to putting her children first. My sister and I always knew that our needs came before our mother's desires. Every year at Christmas, we watched with grateful hearts as our mother worked extra hours to earn additional income to provide a ridiculously abundant Christmas for us. As a result of this sacrificial act and others like it, we grew up knowing that family was critical.

Family must come first; everything else can wait. Nothing, not career, not financial gain, not awards or accolades, nothing is worth sacrificing the family. That community unit must be intact if life is to be worth living. Even in broken homes, those committed to the value of family can be its greatest champions.

(3) Risk Versus Reward

We must ask ourselves, "Is the current path sustainable for the long run?" Every good investor, and especially Warren Buffett, seeks to know whether the current "pricing" is sustainable. They seek to know just how likely a given stock is to rise or fall in light of the "fundamentals." In evaluating our life, we must ask ourselves whether the current path we are on is one that over time will make us or break us. Will it strengthen families or weaken them?

Will the current path enlarge our heart for others and for God, or will it shrink us as a person? Essentially, we must ask, "If I continue on this path, what are the risks?" We must go on to ask, "If I were to embrace God's plan, what would the reward be?" Buffett tells us that when the potential reward far outweighs the risk, then we can, with great confidence, lay down a big bet. To the extent that our reward is assured and our risks minimized, we can "go in big."

Life apart from God is an enormous risk. If Jesus was who He said He was (and there is overwhelming evidence He was), then the rewards of following Him surpass anything this world has to offer. Further, if He was who He said He was, the risks of turning away from Him are enormous and ominous. Can we afford that kind of risk?

(4) The Big Trade/Seize the Day

Occasionally, there comes a time when we are presented with huge opportunities. These opportunities, if taken, can put us on a track we could never have imagined. These open doors, if missed, may never open to us again. Warren Buffett once had the opportunity to buy Coke "on the cheap." He was so sure the trading price was undervalued, and so assured that the future pointed to a much higher price, that he leveraged more than 40 percent of the entire holdings of his company and placed it on that one stock! That would have been an enormous risk if he were not right. The outcome? He made about a billion dollars in a fairly short period of time.

Howard Schultz, in *Pour Your Heart into It*, referring to his success with Starbucks, asserts that life is often about big opportunities missed. Rather than hoping for dumb luck, Schultz suggests that we must pursue our goals with rabid determination and eyes wide open to the internal vision for our future. Rejecting the notion that luck is what separates those who succeed from those who attain their goals, he writes, "It's seizing the day and accepting responsibility for your future. It's seeing what other people don't see, and pursuing that vision, no matter who tells you not to."

Jesus told us He was the way, the truth and the life and that no one comes to God without going through the person of Christ (John 14:6). He told us that He came to earth to offer us abundant life (John 10:10). The biggest deal you will ever make is trading your agenda for His. The most important investment you will ever make is investing the time and effort to seek Him and find that He is who He said He was. You do not know what the next year will bring, the next month, week, day, or even the next hour. Do not put off this trade. The opportunity is there; it may or may not come again. Take Him up on this deal. Sign on the dotted line. Place your life in His hands. Just do it. This decision will make all the difference in your plan to prepare for this life and for the life to come. The rewards, now and forever, are beyond compare.

Finally, I would encourage you to evaluate your life and see if it has a *defining strategy.* Any good investment plan does. You cannot accomplish anything of value without knowing what you are aiming for. Does your strategy make sense? Is it sustainable? Is it self-centered, or does it seek the good of others? Is your game plan worth risking eternity for?

This life offers us many fakes. The mantra, "If it feels good, do it," rings in our ears daily. Does that strategy ultimately make sense? Check the headlines for your answer. When it feels good to strike out in rage, does this strategy work? When grown adults "feel" like misusing their place of power to abuse children, does this strategy work? When husband and wives "feel" like having a fling or two, how does this strategy impact the family? When your son or daughter "feels" like exploring the drug scene, how does the strategy look then? When you have cheated and lied and finally stepped on enough people in business that no one trusts you, how well does the strategy work then? When you say, absolutely, that there is no such thing as absolute truth, how reliable does your strategy look at that point?

Evaluate your strategy. If you find it lacking, it might just be time to make a trade and find another advisor. Jesus said, "Behold, I stand at the door and knock" (Rev. 3:20). Let Him in. There is no better preparedness director you will ever find. He is always on time, He will respond to your cries, and He will carry out His plan for you. The plan to prepare your life begins with knowing Christ.

Purpose in the Storm

Early on in this book, I suggested that God is at work in the storms of life. Whether the storms are sent directly by Him, allowed by Him, or brought in opposition to Him, God's agenda is to accomplish His purposes for us through them. There is much talk in our culture about purpose and the implications for our understanding the purpose of life. Rick Warren's best-selling book, *The Purpose Driven Life,* topped the charts because its message resonates with a longing deep within all of us to know why we are here.

We also long to know why certain storms are brought into our lives. Ultimately, we may never know the answers to some of our questions, but we can know God's purpose for us in a general sense. God's goal for all of us is the same—to build us as people and to bring us into relationship with Him. Just as we need a preparation plan for life, we also need an awareness of what God is up to in the storms we encounter. If we have an awareness of God's will for us amidst the violent squalls, then we will have a steady compass and can make our way through whatever comes our way.

I have listed below a few core values God wants to instill within each of us. These values, once engrained in us, will serve to make us people of immense strength, able to serve under any conditions with grace, compassion, and resolve. It is critical that we come to embrace these core values as early on in life as possible. The sooner they become part of us, the better we will endure the tough stuff we all face. Whenever and wherever we see these qualities exhibited by others, we recognize them and admire them. We ought also to aspire to acquire them.

In order to set the stage for these core values, I need first to address the issue of calling. A sense of calling provides the foundation upon which the core values are built. Without this foundation, the values have no anchor. A sense of calling is the foundation upon which the entire edifice of Christian character is built. If we are to have any motivation to endure the difficulties of life and avoid the allure of sin around us, we must be convinced of the "ultimate why."

Rick Warren challenged millions of readers to base their lives upon a "why," a purpose. The earlier we understand the purpose for which we were created, the earlier we commit ourselves to character development. The earlier we commit ourselves to character development, the sooner we are prepared for the coming soul tsunamis.

Os Guinness, a brilliant author, in his book, *Rising to the Call,* suggests that finding and fulfilling the central purpose of our lives is the fundamental craving deeply rooted in each of us. Few themes, if any, tug at our souls more consistently. Guinness points out that fundamentally we are all asking ourselves how we can find this central purpose in our lives. He writes, "It's a question, of course, but it's more — far, far more. It's a question that's a passion, a longing, a hunger, a restless stirring in our souls, a driving motivation that fires the deepest parts of our lives and taps into the most powerful sources of our energy."

This passion, this deep hunger for our purpose, is fulfilled only by an understanding that we are created for something — and someone. To know early on that we are the apple of God's eye, and that He has specific intentions and plans for us, can and does utterly reorient our lives. I know this truth personally.

This knowledge of God calling us to Himself, and calling us to accomplish certain tasks, builds the corresponding drive for character and gives us strength for any battle that may lie ahead. The lack of such a compelling belief has led to an American culture replete with unfathomable pain amidst enormous wealth. If you doubt this reality, just read the research on the rising crystal meth epidemic in our country. It's a horrifying story of addiction amidst wealth. Guinness points to the problem when he writes, "The trouble is that, as modern people, we have too much to live with and too little to live for."

And so, we must learn just what it is, and who it is, that gives us a reason for living. We must come to understand that the chief end of our lives is to know God and to enjoy Him forever. Once convinced of our calling, we will pursue character. When others see a passionate sense of calling lived out daily in our lives, they will understand and move toward the core values we champion, and our homes, communities, and our world will be better for it. Now, let's get to the core values God wants to instill in each of us.

The Core Values of Life

(1) Courage

God wants us to understand and embrace the pursuit of courage. Big battles will come, and the odds can often seem overwhelming. The courage to look difficulty in the eye and press on is an indispensable trait. Nothing good is accomplished without courage for the fight. Ominous clouds will gather in the days ahead, and the rains will fall, but God stands ready to come to our aid. The knowledge of His keeping power defines us and offers us courage in spite of threatening situations.

(2) The Will to Fight

Some things are worth fighting for. Some battles are pivotal. There are moments in life when we must summon up the resolve to fight for a godly agenda. It may be a fight for fidelity in marriage, a fight for honesty, a fight for friendship, a fight for truth, a fight for financial survival, and more. These fights will come to all of us, and the sooner we learn to fight, the better off we will be. If we fight the integrity battles, and win, we will save ourselves a world of heartache.

(3) Leadership

Amidst the struggles of life, God desires that we learn to develop a focus to point the way for others. We must strive to call others to a better way, a more passionate future. We are called to set the example for others. The value of leadership cannot be overstated. A void in leadership can, and always does, contribute to deterioration of a good plan. All of us have seen examples of good and bad leadership. I have worked alongside those whose leadership demonstrated such an inspiring example of character that nearly everyone around wanted to follow in the direction they were going. Others I have worked with have led those around them into further destruction, moral decay, and selfish ambition. Bad leadership scars our souls. Watching that kind of poor leadership is disheartening, fatiguing, and embarrassing. Leadership for the good inspires us and leads us upward. Leadership amidst crisis can bring us to higher ground.

(4) Character

As we allow God to build character in us, we bless those looking on. Purity, honesty, integrity, compassion, service, and excellence inspire all of us. A humble but passionate pursuit of good goals causes others to jump on board and lend a hand to the mission. Any rebuilding effort worthy of support must begin with leaders who demonstrate character. Any sustaining cause is held together by character. Every life that is worth living is established upon strong character. God's goal in allowing us to go through hard times is the development of our character. Character, simply put, is the ability to consistently do the right thing even when it's not popular.

These core values are derived from an understanding of who we are and to whom we belong. Ultimately, we were created for something, someone, beyond ourselves. Knowledge of the One who created us and who knows the number of hairs on our heads (Matt. 10:30; Luke 12:7) fills us with purpose and direction. Our character depends upon our knowledge of Him. More than knowing about God, we must know Him personally (2 Tim. 1:12). Information will not give us the strength needed to make it through the violent storms we face. What we need is a relationship with the One who can quiet the storms with a whisper.

"This Ain't No Sprint!":
Building for the Long Term

"This ain't no sprint; this is a marathon!" I have heard these words a thousand times since Katrina. In coffee shops, at dinner, in the papers and on television, people are recognizing more and more every day that the rebuilding of New Orleans and the Gulf Coast region will not happen quickly. "Rome was not built in a day, and New Orleans will not be rebuilt in a day," I heard recently. City, state, and federal officials are trumpeting the same message: It's going to be a long road back.

No doubt, we are in for a long, hard run in this rebuilding effort. This is going to take a great deal of time and a huge dose of endurance. I cannot help but think, however, how much of this grief we could have avoided here in New Orleans had the construction crews, engineers, and leadership prepared our levees for the long run. What seems sure now is that the extensive flooding that overcame New Orleans was a result of poor levee construction. The levees, it seems, were constructed with materials that, over time, broke down, leaving weak spots in critical places. Those weak spots gave way in the worst of times, and the results were devastating.

What if New Orleans' levees had been constructed with materials known to have the ability to maintain their integrity for a much longer period of time? What if the levees had been built to withstand a Category-Five hurricane rather than just a Category-Three storm? Amidst the rubble now, the answers to these questions are clear and frustrating. As is the case with this physical destruction, so it is with our lives. When we plan, prepare, and build a life for the long term, we win. When we make our decisions and construct our lives upon the short term, the momentary, we fail, and destruction ensues. Further, when our decisions — or life's circumstances — have led to a need to rebuild, we must at that point make a conscious decision to rebuild for the long haul.

My goal in the next few pages is to offer a model for building or rebuilding a life, a community, a city, or a country for the long term. The marathon runner offers us some helpful insights into this endurance challenge. As any accomplished marathoner is aware, a successful race requires much more than the unbridled enthusiasm and inspiration felt while at the starting line. If the distance runner is going to make it to the end and reach his goal, certain natural abilities have to be developed and nurtured.

I believe the lessons here will be helpful to anyone looking to gain a fresh start. Though the goal may seem to be a long way off, with proper training, conditioning, and care, it is possible to make it to the finish line. Not only that, it is possible to run the race and finish well. With proper training, nutrition, and care, the race can be a rewarding one. Let's take a look at the keys to staying in the race and enjoying the competition.

Keys to Making It Through the Marathon of Life

(1) Learn to adapt to race-day conditions.

Strong marathoners prepare themselves to run in any conditions. Even in overwhelming heat, good marathoners will be able to adapt and indeed thrive in the race. As people searching for our way in the disasters of life, we need to find the resolve that enabled Shadrac and his friends to remain in the fiery furnace waiting for God to show up (Dan. 3:8-30). The heat will be turned up at times in our lives. If we choose to give up each time a major challenge comes our way, we give up on the call of God to make us what He is calling us to be.

Jeremiah was called the "weeping prophet," but he endured the hardships and heartaches to become God's great spokesman. Do not forsake the race of faith when everyone around you appears to be caving in. Endure the heat, adapt to conditions, and run for your life. When conditions around you are less than favorable, take courage, look up, and keep running. There is a reward at the end.

(2) Beat muscle soreness.

The race will take its toll at times. You may feel beat up. But as any athlete knows, muscle soreness is a sign you are doing things right and growth is taking place. Don't quit when the soreness sets in. Work through it, and allow God to bring about the growth He intends. It's part of the process. There is no better feeling than to know you just gave it your all, played your heart out, and left the field exhausted but exhilarated because of your effort. Run through the tough spots; keep your stride. It hurts at times, but remember: While pain may last for the night, joy comes in the morning (Ps. 30:5). The only way to get rid of the soreness is to keep on keeping on. Keep building.

(3) Learn to train in the pain.

Press through the workouts even when you feel some pain. All great runners, and, indeed, all great athletes, "play hurt" from time to time. Who can forget those nights when Michael Jordan came to the court totally depleted, dehydrated, and weak, and yet played his heart out and scored fifty points to lead his team to a big win? Those kinds of moments inspire onlookers. They are unforgettable. When you are pressing hard for the goal, there will be moments when you hurt. Stay with it, keep running, and never, never, never give up. When you are rebuilding and giving every ounce of energy you have, sometimes you can lose focus and drive that hammer right into your thumb. The expletives come, and the pain throbs. But keep hammering away. A few more nails, and you may just have yourself a house.

(4) Make use of massage therapy.

Marathon runners have many massages during their training period. Without this kind of professional care and attention, their muscles would not last for the next day of training. Massage, attention to muscle soreness, is critical for muscle repair and functioning. None of us, no matter how "spiritual," can go it alone all the time. We all need some help occasionally. At times, even leaders need to consult someone who can offer counseling and help for issues they wrestle with.

There are no Christian supermen. Rather than pretend you are something you are not, get help when you need it. It's okay to ask for assistance. God intends for us to minister to one another. Left unattended, some of our issues, hurts, and pains will scar us for life and destroy the life of God within us. Everyone in Katrina's reach was affected. Rich, poor, middle class, and people of every color, shape, size, and age felt her wrath. Too many, however, try to hide behind money, position, accomplishment, or a spiritual façade to mask the fear and uncertainty. None of us can go it alone all the way; all of us need someone else to give us a hand or lend us an ear occasionally.

We were created for community, and we die when we do not have it. That's why few runners run alone. There is strength in numbers. Get some care when you need it. When your arms are heavy from lifting too many rafters, call for some "arch support."

(5) Follow injury recovery strategies.

It is not true that "time heals all wounds." Some wounds, left alone, only get worse. Scar tissue can hinder proper function in the body. Runners pay special attention to hip, back, and knee issues. If they neglect an injury to one of these areas too long, it can indeed take them out of the race. These are important factors for runners. Marathoners cannot endure twenty-six miles with a major problem in one of these critical areas. As builders, we must address the important issues in our lives. Those besetting sins that we hide from others can ultimately sideline us.

Take care of the nasty wounds and get a bandage on them as quickly as you can. Properly cared for, they can heal and gain new strength. Neglected, they can put you on the disabled list. And if you are on the disabled list, you cannot be a difference maker; you cannot run the race of life. Bitterness is not the proper response to the events in life you consider unfair. Surrendering to the forces that are battering you is not the way to victory either. Allow God to bind up your wounds and get you running again.

(6) Maintain proper nutrition.

Maintaining a proper diet is absolutely critical for distance runners. The right mix of fat, carbohydrates, and protein is essential to performance. If runners eat too much fat or too few carbs leading into race day, they will not perform as well as they should. Likewise, as people attempting to rebuild, if we do not feed on the Word of God daily, we will falter, wear out, and lose momentum. Being fed on Sunday is not enough. We must place ourselves at God's training table on a daily basis. Remember, the chief end of man is to know God and enjoy Him forever. We cannot know Him if we are not spending time learning of Him and from Him on a regular basis. If we do not know Him, then we cannot enjoy Him. If we are not enjoying Him, we will not have the emotional capacity to stay in the race when the challenges of the course come.

Following a drive-through philosophy is the same as feeding on the fad-foods of the day. Like sugar, it will bring a quick high, but ultimately, a huge crash. Jesus said that He is the way, the truth, and the life, and suggested that no one comes to God apart from Him (John 14:6). He is the fuel on which we are meant to run our race—the race of life. When tempted to give up on the rebuilding effort, when you find yourself too tired to get up another day, open His Word and get the nutrition you need to keep at it.

(7) Keep a training log.

Runners oftentimes keep a very accurate journal of performance. Seconds shaved can make a difference. Adjustments in technique can save long-distance runners precious minutes in a race. Accomplishments and goals pursued and recorded offer ongoing incentive to runners to keep on track with the training process. As long-term builders we find great hope when we can look back on what God has done in our lives, the lessons we have learned along the way, and the challenges we have navigated in the past. These records of performance give us passion to remain in the race and pursue the finish line.

This race in which we are involved is not a sprint. Keeping that fact in mind, we must recognize that our memory tends to fade over the long haul. Keep track of those key moments when you know that God gave you the extra spark you needed to stay in the race. In the future, when fatigue and discouragement set in, you may need these reminders of God's care and providence.

We must pursue rebuilding our life in the same way runners pursue the finish line; it is a goal worth pursuing (1 Cor. 9:24-25). Remember: Our reward is eternal, and the joy set before us is our inspiration. Run to show the life of God in you. Pursue the finish with the same enthusiasm with which you started. In fact, make it your prayer that God will enable you to sprint through the finish line! Be faithful, finish well, and build your life better than it was before.

Storm Memorials

Our nation is filled with important monuments: the Lincoln Memorial, the Vietnam Veterans Memorial, Mount Rushmore, the Statue of Liberty, and many more. The significance of these monuments lies in the critical "moment" in American history that they represent or the American values they point toward. I have had the privilege to view many of these monuments, and each one has inspired me in a different way. One of the most emotional for me was the Lincoln Memorial and the marble slab just in front of its entrance, a tribute to Martin Luther King Jr. and his famous "I have a dream" speech.

Just as our nation has many memorials of great significance, each of us has important moments in our lives that we ought to memorialize. The work of God on our behalf in critical moments should not be taken lightly or forgotten. Throughout scripture, the people of God named places and set monuments in places where God "showed up." Each name, each place became an important landmark in the life of God's people for generations to come. As the stories were told around these landmarks, new generations came to understand the intimate nature of God's involvement with His people. The same should be true of us today.

Katrina and the various storms of our lives offer us moments where God breaks in and makes us aware of His provision and care for us. Where has God showed up for you? When, where, and how did He impart His grace, strength, compassion, provision, or mercy when you desperately needed it? What strength and visible demonstration of His hand did God extend to you amidst the storm? Have you memorialized it? Have you told others about it?

We all like to "collect" certain memorabilia. For some, it's photos; for others, it's sports cards or autographed balls. I love sports memorabilia and have a number of items of some value, each pointing toward a particular moment in sports history or the character of a great athlete. But my most important "monuments" are those items I keep around me that point to God's active involvement in my life. One of those monuments to God's grace that I keep on my desk is a softball given to me years ago by an older mentor who pitched on our church softball team. I keep that ball because as a teenager I came to faith after watching this man's life and the lives of many others in my church over a long period of time. I played shortstop, and the pitcher would regularly give out a Most Valuable Player ball for defense after games. The balls were embossed with the initials S.T.O.P. (Saved The Old Pitcher), and yes, I collected quite a few! The point is that God showed up for me as a teenager and won me over on those softball fields as I watched the life of God lived out in the hearts of this man and others on the field. The ball is a monument to God's hand in my life.

Here's the crucial point for us as believers and as storm survivors. God is indeed intimately aware of our difficulties, accomplishments, failures, and successes. He moves on our behalf. He has our good in mind. He is designing our lives. He will not allow anything to separate us from His love (Rom. 8:35-39).

Just as in the case of Joseph, though many "pits" come our way and though many conspire against us for our demise, God has our good in mind. Just as in the life of David, though our own strength may not match that of our oppressors, God's strength is enough to defeat the giants in our lives. Just as He did with the woman at the well, He breaks through those barriers that keep us from abundant life, and He offers us living water. Just as He did for the woman caught in adultery, He silences our would-be prosecutors and extends us grace when we do not deserve it.

The very stones others intend for our destruction He uses to establish and build monuments of beauty in our lives. How many times must Peter have gone back to those shores next to the very waters where God allowed him to walk where no other human had ever walked? How many times must the woman caught in adultery have gone back to that courtyard of grace where her life was spared? I have a hunch she may have kept one of those rocks for the rest of her life.

When God extends His hand on our behalf, we ought to memorialize it in our hearts. We ought, also, to memorialize those moments in some way physically as well: write it down, keep that photo, place that memento somewhere prominent, memorialize that piece of debris, and by all means, tell the story to others.

Just as our national monuments are physical reminders of stories of courage and devotion, so we as Christians ought to have visible benchmarks to remind us to tell our stories of God's love and grace! We need to cherish the work God has done in us and for us, and to mark it in some way. These monuments are the glue that adheres us to His purposes when the going gets tough. These monuments call us to taste and see that the Lord is good (Ps. 34:8).

The Church:
Levee and Shelter from the Storm

National Public Radio's coverage of Hurricane Katrina and the rebuilding efforts in New Orleans included a feature on Emergency Medical Service workers and their reports of the massive increase in suicide rates and psychological trauma. The emergency workers interviewed told of suicide rates in New Orleans doubling in the months following the storm. Though the population of the city has diminished by at least one-third and perhaps by as much as 50 percent, the number of suicides and attempted suicides continues to rise. In the months following the storm, distress call levels each day matched what would have been weekly totals prior to the storm.

One of the disturbing accounts given during the NPR interview was that of an elderly woman who was left behind by her family when they evacuated. Intoxicated, depressed, and without hope, this woman went to her kitchen, turned on the gas at the stove, and then sat down in a chair to die.

EMS workers told NPR that these kinds of things were happening every day throughout the city. The darker reality is that even these heroic emergency workers were not immune to the soul-wrenching pain brought by Katrina. Many of them lost their own homes and yet had to spend long hours helping others, leaving little time to deal with their own issues.

One EMS worker named Paul told of his battle with depression. Paul shared his grief with radio listeners, telling of his struggle with the overwhelming sadness that blanketed his soul. Daily, he would sit alone and weep. Paul went on to share that his mind was so overcome by the emotional stress that he often forgot where he was and why he had ventured to a certain part of town while running errands and tending to his own business.

Where are people to find hope when everything around them is in shambles? Is there any protection from the soul tsunami that threatens to bring more destruction as each day passes? Where does one turn to find help for the challenge of removing the debris inside, which clutters the heart and overwhelms the emotions? The good news is that God has given us a protection system, and He has provided shelter from the storms of life. That shelter and protection is to be found in the church. By this I do not mean, simply, the four walls of a building. Rather, the church is the community of faith devoted to God and living daily life out of a passionate and authentic attempt to honor Him and do His will His way.

Shelter in the Early Church:
Acts 2

Acts 2 offers us an amazing view of what it is like to know, love, and serve God in community. The image offered is one that provides a source of healing and protection for people like Paul and anyone else who has been confronted with life's cruel realities. The church, as revealed in the book of Acts, is a testimony to what God can do in the world when people are willing to take Him at His word and live according to His plan. It is a picture of selflessness, provision, friendship, and support. Those early believers, who had just endured the disaster of seeing their Leader crucified, had come to know the hope and new life offered through the resurrection, and found the promise of a better life.

The description of the church in the book of Acts demonstrates how a relationship with God, in community with others, can lead to a life that promotes emotional, psychological, and spiritual health. It is a testimony to the church's call and ability to be an influence for properly functioning communities. Let's take a look at the inspiring picture of the church in community in Acts 2:42-47:

> And they devoted themselves to the apostle's teaching and fellowship, to the breaking of bread and to prayer. And awe came upon every soul, and many wonders and signs were being done through the apostles. And all who believed were together and had all things in common. And they were selling their possessions and belongings and distributing the proceeds to all, as any had need. And day by day, attending the temple together and breaking bread in their homes, they received their food with glad and generous hearts, praising God and having favor with all the people. And the Lord added to their number day by day those who were being saved.

I don't know that I can ever read that passage without being moved toward great aspiration and a hunger for that kind of community. Each time I read that text, something happens in me. For me, that is one of the special "moments" captured in scripture that causes the hairs to stand up on the back of the neck and gets the goose bumps popping. Don't we all hunger for that kind of existence? That is the way life was meant to be.

The passage tells us that as the church goes about its business, the result is awe. I don't know about you, but I have seen too much in the church that is far from awe-inspiring; *awful* is a more apt description. But we have the promise that the church can function appropriately, and the result will be that those looking in on its activity will be drawn to it. The life of the church, the unselfishness demonstrated by the early church, gave hope and inspiration to every soul within reach. Those living around us need to see the life-transforming power of the church in order to find shelter from the storm and protection from the floodwaters. The church is to be a levee for the world. We are called to keep at bay those forces that seek to bring havoc to our communities and our world.

The early believers had everything in common! This is a big one. One of the major stumbling blocks for nonbelievers coming to the church for help is the fact that they see far too much lack of commonality among churchgoers. It remains true today that the most segregated hour in American society is the Sunday morning church hour. It should not be. If we are ever to see a society in which the issues surrounding race are overcome, it must begin with the church. Government, politics, and all the other initiatives out there have no hope in redressing this wrong. It can be resolved only as God brings reconciliation through the church. All the battles over reparations will never bring a resolution. Reconciliation is the answer. Black and white, Jew and Gentile, rich and poor, and people of every other stripe will find peace only through the common denominator of knowing, loving, and serving God.

In the weeks and months following the devastation on the Gulf Coast, the church has come alive. Thousands of church volunteers from across the country and the world have rushed into the area to bring food, supplies, and encouragement. While FEMA and our government found the task too huge to handle, it was the church that showed up, without delay, and provided much-needed help for those in desperate situations. Church workers from far and wide came to build, hand out food, give money, provide medical care, and offer comfort. The surroundings did not matter to them as they ministered. For days, weeks, and months, they came and slept on the floors of churches, in tents, in campers, and on cots in temporary shelters. The help continues to pour in as day after day the church extends its provisions to any who have need.

The world needs the church. The church, the Bride of Christ, is the hope of the world. As the church fulfills the role God intended for her, she finds favor, people respond, and communities are transformed. This is God's process for changing our world. As the people of God walk with authenticity and live life from a compassionate perspective, God adds daily to the ranks of those finding meaning, significance, hope, and purpose.

Protection for Our Communities: The Levee

> Man's accidents are God's purposes.
> —Sophia Hawthorne

As we now know, the breaking of the levees surrounding New Orleans led to widespread destruction. A staggering 80 percent of the New Orleans metro area was flooded when the protection system gave way. Without protection, cities fall. Without the protection of the church, souls, cities, and nations crumble.

America, the "nation under God," now finds herself amidst a tempestuous soul storm. Our culture is in moral decay. Though it is not recognized by many, the devastation around us resembles the devastation on the Gulf Coast. Through various media, every day, we hear over and over again stories that, if we were not so jaded and calloused, would defy our imagination. Violence and immorality run rampant in our culture. Even so, the media and those in opposition to the idea of absolute truth, continue to champion the moral failings that are leading to our demise.

Just as the studies were ignored that predicted the failure of the New Orleans protection systems, America seems to be turning a deaf ear to the growing body of research that points to the failure of any society that abandons principles of truth and goodness. Our country needs to be reminded of the protection granted as the church is given a voice in the national building process. If we continue to ignore the warnings, we do so at our own peril. God's design for the proper functioning of communities demands that the church be involved.

I make these suggestions while recognizing that the church does not and has not always gotten it right. Too often, God's people operate in ways that bring shame upon the reputation of the church. History is, of course, replete with examples of the church at work in opposition to God's agenda. Individually and corporately, God's people have acted in ways that, rather than leading those looking in to stand in awe, have led them to turn away in disgust.

Recognizing that the church does not always get it right does not deny the reality that God intends for His church to be the protection system for the world. We saw the desperation of those in governmental leadership as they made attempt after attempt to handle the aftermath of Katrina. Eventually, those in leadership cried out for the help of the church. When the church showed up and went to work, these leaders stood in awe and often told of the critical role she played in bringing much-needed relief in a time of unprecedented panic. We must recognize the central importance of the church in our world. Those of us in the church must heed the call of God to operate as a biblically functioning community. We must engage our world. We cannot run from society.

God's desire and plan for His church is that she be a transforming influence. Historically, the church has had trouble coming to grips with her God-given role. She has viewed herself as standing above culture. At other times, the church has positioned herself in opposition to culture.

The pitfall of "fundamentalism" is that in adopting it the church becomes so removed from society or so pitted against it that no transforming influence is exerted. There is a balance that must be struck. The church cannot and must not accommodate society and so resemble it that nothing of value is offered. Capitulation to the whims of society has left many church groups in massive decline for decades. When a church becomes little more than a social club or an entertainment enterprise, God exits the building. No matter what the sign outside says, if God is not present no church exists. The goal of the church must be to find an Acts 2 model that extends God's presence, influence, compassion, and relevance, and thus brings awe to communities.

One of the churches my family and I attended in Dallas after Katrina was Oak Cliff Bible Fellowship, where Pastor Tony Evans preaches. Dr. Evans' first message after the storm, a message given to a full house with hundreds of evacuees present, addressed the call of the church to be the levee God intended. When we Christians fail to live lives of purity, sobriety, compassion, and devotion, we weaken the protection system. To the extent that the church is weakened, our society becomes vulnerable to catastrophe. If the church will not be the model that God intended, how can she have any hope of transforming the culture that surrounds her?

Just as the integrity of New Orleans' levees led to the demise of a great city, the breakdown in the integrity of God's people will lead to a further deterioration in the moral condition of our country. If our nation is to have a bright future, the church must strengthen herself so that the country might have the resources to endure the storms ahead. Will the church be a place of refuge should the avian flu pandemic become a reality? Will the church be a place of shelter should race relations deteriorate so far that violence erupts in our streets at levels previously unseen? Can the church so closely resemble the Acts 2 model that she fends off potential disaster? It can happen. It must happen. Remember: As God's chosen instrument, the church, and only the church, is the hope of the world.

Debris Removal:
Healing in the Church

If you take time to drive through any street or neighborhood in New Orleans or anywhere along the Gulf Coast where Katrina came ashore, you will see mountains of debris. In some areas, the piles of rubble are twenty feet high. What is sobering to remember as you drive past the mountains of rubbish is the reality that each pile represents a home, a family, a dream, a shattered life. The sheer volume of it all is hard to fathom. How can a disaster be so far-reaching and so severe?

The images we have all seen on television point to a deeper reality in human experience. Far too many souls resemble the ruins that remain in areas hit by Hurricane Katrina. I have known and loved a number of people who have made choices so destructive that the emotional, physical, and psychological devastation has left them imprisoned. Anyone who has seen the consequences of addiction, bitterness, rage, and relational recklessness knows of inner turmoil.

A question arises from the mess left by Katrina and from our struggles with our own inner chaos: Where do we turn for debris removal? In New Orleans, even months later, enormous challenges remain in the effort to get rid of all of the debris. Where will it all go? Who will pay the bill for the work? How long is the cleanup going to take? When life turns ugly, and we have made a mess of things, similar questions arise: How and where do we find healing? Who can help us through this dark night of the soul? Is there any hope, any forgiveness, any restoration? Can we ever get over this disaster?

Billy Graham has suggested that a large percentage of those in mental institutions could be healed and released if they would just come to God and find forgiveness from the guilt tormenting them. While I am no psychologist or psychiatrist, I do agree that many people suffer in mental and emotional anguish as a result of the miserable choices they have made. I have witnessed this fact as people I care for have gone the way of the Prodigal Son and have found themselves living among pigs (Luke 15:11-19). Rather than turning and running back to God, too many have chosen to remain in the muck and filth, wallowing in emotional, physical, mental, and spiritual chaos.

While I am certain that there are many in our society who truly need professional care for mental illness and chemical imbalance issues, I am equally sure that many could find peace and healing in turning to God and the Christian community. God has designed us with a need for Him and a deep longing for a relationship with Him and with others. Social scientists have known for years that one of our most basic needs is for human relationships.

We have all felt the pain and disillusionment of watching the church at its worst. There is no denying that the church is filled with imperfect people. It is also true, however, that the church has many great moments. There is nothing like witnessing firsthand the power and grace of God at work in the midst of a people radically committed to Him. It just does not get any better than that.

When the church is operating as God intended, it is something to behold. That is what was taking place in the book of Acts. It still happens today. Stories continue to be told every day in and around New Orleans about the activity of churches and their efforts to bring relief to those hit hard by the storm. Churches from around the world have come to bring supplies, money, medical equipment, clothing, and food. It seems that there is no end to their generosity. This is in stark contrast to reports being told about the limitations of governmental agencies. CNN.com recently reported for example that a dire situation has developed in the handful of months since the storm:

> Months after Hurricane Katrina forces tens of thousands from their homes, bureaucracy is creating a new tide of trouble for storm victims. "We feel like we are citizens of the United States who are nearly forgotten," said Governor Kathleen Blanco.

There exists no agency, government, or institution that has

enough resources or ability to reach all those impacted by life's toughest challenges. Eventually, all the resources of mankind fall short in dealing with issues of the soul. Only God has enough resources to meet our deepest needs. His plan is to extend those resources through His Bride, the church. We are instructed in scripture not to forsake meeting together for worship and fellowship (Heb. 10:25). Why? Because in the church, in true community, God has arranged for our cry amidst destruction, disruption, and displacement to be heard by others who know, love, and serve Him. This is where we find the strength to go on. This is where we find the answers we seek. This is where, by God's design, we find others to walk through the dark valleys of life with us.

I can remember a time when the church really came through for my family and me when I was a young, poor, and struggling graduate student. At the time, I was married, had two children, and was working in a small church and attending school forty minutes from home. We had one car to provide for the transportation needs of a family of four who had to be going in different directions during the day. Living on food stamps, Medicaid, student loans, and a very small stipend, it was tough to make ends meet. With no options, and getting desperate, we turned to the church we were attending, and God responded to our needs through them.

When we shared our need for transportation, we were thrilled to find out that the church had an entire ministry devoted to people like us. The C.A.R.S. ministry was set up to provide reliable transportation for needy families with no other remedy. The generosity of those in the church with more than enough resources made this dream a reality. Those in the church who could afford to purchase a new car without trading in their old one actually donated their old car to the church to give to those in need. Just as in the book of Acts, those who had, shared with those who did not.

Similar stories coming from those finding their needs met in and around the Gulf Coast offer a testimony to the power of community. Such life-giving community is found, by God's design, in the church. In this design, those who are experiencing a life of abundance find the thrill of giving back, and those who are struggling to find God in their misery are surprised by the grace expressed through the love of others. The plan works.

The church is also God's redemptive agency for soul relief. We need His church and radically loving communities of faith at work in our nation and in our world. If you are looking to rebuild your life, if you are looking for help in removing the debris that clutters your soul, if you are looking for life-giving relationships, turn to God and get involved in His church. The church is the hope of the world. Your future, my future, and the future of our cities, nation, and world depend upon the leadership of the church.

CONCLUDING REMARKS: GOD AND DISASTER

Rome was not built in a day.

— Popular saying

The Perfect Storm: The Fat Pitch

We have been told that Rome was not built in a day. Neither are storms. Meteorologists have known for some time just how many factors must come together in order for a Category-Five storm to develop. Unlike a thunderstorm or a spring shower, Category-Five hurricanes are grand in scale and complicated in design. Wind patterns, water temperatures, jet streams, eye wall development, front positions, and system speed must all combine in a specific recipe if a storm is to reach its full potential. In the case of Katrina, the recipe was a potent mix.

Our lives, much like the perfect storm, are a complicated mixture of circumstances and events. Yet the circumstances and events of our lives do not occur randomly nor do they stand alone. On the contrary, the relationships we choose, the decisions we make, the worldviews we embrace, and the passions of our heart all have an impact upon the unfolding of our story. The good, the bad, and the ugly in our lives are not independent realities. It all adds up, and it is all leading us somewhere. Occasionally, in moments of great clarity, we can see the events of our lives leading to a critical "moment" or "juncture," the proverbial "fork in the road."

Studies suggest that for many people, if not most, intense storms in life often serve as those hinge events that shape the rest of their time spent here on this planet. Watching a close loved one die can totally alter a person psychologically, emotionally, relationally, and spiritually. A romance gone awry can scar an individual for life. The loss of great wealth, loss of a limb, loss of a job, loss of a home, and loss of any kind often changes the landscape of an individual's soul in dramatic fashion. All these kinds of things and others cause people to change.

Here is the good news. Often these trying events, these storms of the soul, serve to direct people toward greater things. As we have heard, "What doesn't kill you makes you stronger." It is true, as we have seen in the pages of this book, that tragedy and great challenge can be "the very thing the doctor ordered," assuming, of course, that the doctor is the Great Physician. The outcome, we must be aware, is contingent upon our determination to find God and His purposes in the events of our lives. Those people who do take note of His hand and embrace His agenda are the ones who will find the life they always wanted riding upon the storms of life. Viewed with a divine perspective, the soul tsunami becomes the moment they've always dreamed of. But they must see the opportunity. And seize it.

Ted Williams, the Baseball Hall of Famer, was a consummate batter, known for his prowess at the plate. No one has ever matched his hitting percentage. And it is very doubtful that anyone ever will. As a junior in high school, Williams attained a breathtaking hitting percentage of .583. In 1941 he posted a major league batting percentage of .400, and it has not been matched since. That is astounding performance in a sport where the batter's task is to hit a small round object flying toward him at speeds in excess of ninety miles per hour. To make matters more challenging, the batter, of course, loses his opportunity after only three misses. More challenging yet, the batter, the one at whom the miniature missles are being launched, is confined to a very small box in which all of this drama unfolds. So, how does a player with these challenges and disadvantages develop a winning strategy? He does so with his eyes.

Ted Williams, as baseball lovers are aware, was not only a great hitter, he was a great teacher. His instructions for hitting are as good as they come, and the lessons he taught for successful hitting have many parallels to life. His first piece of advice for hitters applies to vision: The ability to see the situation as it really is determines success or failure at the plate and in life. If you cannot see what is developing, there is no hope in getting wood on the ball. And if wood and ball never meet, you strike out, you lose.

Early on, the hitter must develop the ability to see where the ball is headed. The parallel for living is clear. The earlier in life we develop the ability to "see" where our lives are headed, the better off we will be. If our life continually appears to be headed toward the outside portion of the plate, the area of the strike zone most difficult to hit, we must ask ourselves why. If we continually say to ourselves, "I didn't see that one coming," we need to reevaluate our stance and our perspective. If our hitting percentage in relationships, work, emotional health, and inner peace continues to fall, we need to have our eyes checked. Are we looking at life the wrong way?

The vision of a hitter, however, is not confined to the eyes, Ted Williams points out. In the end, it comes down to feel. Williams had 20/10 vision, as do many excellent hitters. But what separated him from the others is the fact that he "felt" when he swung. That sensation, which told him he had found the "sweet spot," is what he was looking for.

That feeling is one that any good athlete craves. Tennis players remember those days when the ball just "comes off the racquet the right way" every time. Runners remember those days when they hit that "runner's high" or find the "runner's stride." And basketball players thirst for those moments when they feel like they "just can't miss." When it's not happening, athletes are constantly asking themselves, "How do I find it?" For the competitor in any sport, not having "it" brings great frustration.

How does your life "feel"? That's a very different question from what you might at first think. Deep inside your soul, when you are alone, when you are looking inside the person you, and only you, know that you are, how does your life "feel"? Have you hit the "sweet spot"? Are you living life as it was intended to be lived? Do you know, in those few honest moments, that something is missing? If you can answer those questions honestly, your "fat pitch" may be on the way.

Seeing and feeling are two critical components to hitting. The most important part of the equation, however, is the pitch. "The pitch?" you might say. "But that's outside of the hitter's control! How can good hitting be determined by something that is clearly outside of the hitter's hands? That's unfair!" But is it? What if some people get better pitches than others? "But what if the pitcher is lousy and never gets the ball over the plate? Sometimes, don't you just have to swing at anything?"

This is where Ted Williams' hitting strategy has its most direct application to our discussion in this book. His teaching on hitting, while it addressed varied facets of the swing and a player's individual technique, found its great strength in its focus on choosing the right pitch to hit. Great hitters, contrary to popular belief, don't hit just any pitch well. Those with high hitting percentages pick their pitches carefully and only swing when the pitch is "ripe."

The pitch is the deal. What kind of pitch does a great hitter look for? What kind of "set up" are we to look for in life? How do we know what to do when we see a good pitch? It comes down to seeing, perceiving, and knowing when the time is at hand to swing, and to swing big. When the pitch headed our way is clearly a ripe one, it is time to swing with all our might.

Ted Williams' hitting strategy encourages hitters to only swing big when the pitch is one that falls in their strongest hitting "cell." That cell varies for each hitter. Not every player is happy with the same kind of pitch. Certain pitches, while good for one hitter, may not be the "fat" one for another hitter. At the plate, and in life, we have to know when and where the situation has brought *us* to our hitting zone. We have to know when it is time for us to swing. We must be able to see the pitch setting up for us. Reminding us of the importance of the right pitch, Ted suggests, "All hitters have areas they like to hit in. But you can't beat the fact that you've got to get a good ball to hit."

"A good ball to hit." Warren Buffett refers to it as the "fat pitch." He writes, "To succeed in investing or in writing insurance, you have wait for the fat pitch." In baseball, in investing, and in life we are occasionally thrown the pitch we have always sought. At that moment we have to apply another of Ted Williams' hitting principles and swing quick and hard. I call it "swinging for the fence." No one gets a bunch of those kinds of pitches, so when one does show up, the swing must be fierce. This is the kind of pitch that Buffett swings at when he sees a ripe investment opportunity. As he suggests, when the deck is stacked in your favor, lay down a big bet.

What is known of Ted Williams is that he would swing only when he was thrown a pitch in that fat "cell," as he called it. That discipline, and that determination to swing away at opportune moments, set him apart from the rest. If we are willing to apply such a strategy to life, it can and will make all the difference for us.

Here, now, is the point of this little lesson in baseball hitting theory. The storms of life provide us with the fat pitch more than we realize. Because our sight is often blinded by improper focus, we often fail to see the pitch coming. God sends, allows, or directs the floodwaters our way in order to get our attention. While it may look bad at first, in actuality He is setting us up for our greatest day at the plate. Though the trials may appear to have us down in the count, we still have one more swing left. The issue at hand is what we will do with the swing that remains. It is time for us as individuals, as communities, and as a nation to choke up on the bat, quicken our swing, and find the sweet spot. If we are to hit a home run, and begin to pursue life as it is intended, we must see the pitch now coming our way — it's a fat one.

Is Katrina, as difficult as the challenges she has brought are, the pitch we needed here in America? Are the questions she raises in our minds as individuals the beginning of our quest to see life from God's point of view? Can we find our sweet spot amidst such heartache? I think we can. This could very well be the moment we've longed for. For a nation that is losing its way, Katrina could be our wake-up call. What has happened to the "Christian" nation? It is not much of a stretch to acknowledge that we have lost our way, especially if we take time to consider the present commitment of political and community leaders and retail merchandising chains to remove the word "Christmas" from all public expressions and advertising for the "holiday" season. How unthinkable that we may soon be celebrating a "holiday" with no foundations! What will we then be celebrating, and why?

As has been said before, we are educating ourselves into imbecility. Should it surprise anyone that we are seeing the rate and severity of crisis increase within our nation? Addictions, broken homes, sexually transmitted diseases, violence, poverty, racial tensions, financial scandal, political corruption, and other devastating realities are most certainly not abating in our society. Is there any link to our inability to "see" life as it ought to be viewed?

The recent events on the Gulf Coast ought to be viewed as a fresh opportunity to reevaluate who we are as a people. The storms of our own life should be viewed as a means of renewed spiritual fervor. No one who has ever turned to God amidst disaster has found Him wanting.

If you are a political leader who, perhaps, has witnessed the devastation on the Gulf Coast, and has seen in stark terms just how short the arm of government is when it comes to reaching people in their pain, maybe this is your time to see your role and your heart in a different light. Could it be that it is time to turn from a desire for selfish political power and gain to a desire for true influence and impact?

If you are a husband or wife who has found yourself "at play" in the soiled sheets of a hotel bed or a "romantic hideout," perhaps the soul storm in which you find yourself is your call to come home. Never has any man or woman found that missing part of the soul in the arms of another human being. As John Eldredge points out in his book *Wild at Heart,* the attempt to answer the deepest questions of a man's heart through the pursuit of "Eve" will always turn up empty.

However severe may be the storm that rages in your heart, God is willing to respond. Have you found yourself drowning in the shallow waters of pleasure, money, and fame? Has the fulfillment of all your wildest fantasies still left you lacking? If so, perhaps it's time to admit, along with Solomon, the wisest man who ever lived, that all of this seeking after material gratification is "meaningless, a chasing after the wind" (Eccl. 1:14 NIV). The storm will not subside until you do. Whether you are trapped in the shackles of a selfish life or caged in the prison of poverty or social injustice, the message is the same for you and for everyone—God is able (Rom. 4:20-21). The present storm does not have to be your ultimate undoing. This can be your chance to hit a "grand slam."

Hurricane Katrina, as nasty as she was, has provided for many the route to a better life. Some of the evacuees forced to leave their homes have been given the fat pitch of new opportunity. Those who take advantage and ride the winds to a new day will thank Katrina in the end. Looking back, years from now, many will be able to give testimony to this storm's divine ability to get them to the Promised Land. Like Louis Braille, who through a tragic accident with an awl went blind in both eyes at the age of three and went on to create the Braille system of reading for the blind, many will seize the opportunity afforded by Katrina to dream new dreams and conquer new territory.

The critical issue at hand concerns America's response to this historic "natural" disaster. What will we do with Katrina's message? How will we view this event? Do we have the sharpness of eyes to see and the quickness of conscience to swing, and swing for the fence? This may be our fat pitch. We would do well to remember that pitches like this one don't come very often. Is this our perfect storm? It could be. The answer may depend on how we respond to the call.

The Call for America to Change

NBC news anchor Brian Williams recently commented on the impact of Hurricane Katrina on him by saying, "This has changed my life forever . . . and it ought to change our country and the way we think about class, race, and social issues." He went on to say that the faces, the anguish, the depth of despair, and the images of chaos will remain in his mind for a long time. Months after the storm, he and many others who covered the disaster still find themselves thinking about it late into the night while trying to sleep. Hurricane Katrina, indeed, has changed everything for all of us. Williams stated that this disaster ought to change the way we think about important social issues, and I agree. Further, change ought to take place deep within us in relation to our thinking about faith issues and our relationship with God and others.

If we as Americans fail to ponder the meaning and significance of such events and run back to our obsessions with pleasure, money, success, and accomplishment, we are destined to a future of emptiness, and we remain vulnerable to bigger storms to come. In the winds and waters of Katrina, God is calling us back to Himself. Through such events, God reveals to us the insufficiency of living for ourselves with no thought of Him or others. These kinds of catastrophes ought to serve to call us to recognize the frailty and poverty of embracing a distorted view of life that causes us to run after that which ultimately entraps us. As a culture, we have been duped into believing that bad is good and good is bad. We have fallen for a lie. The result is a nation full of souls in disarray and a national conscience cluttered with debris.

Like Isaiah, we must see evil for what it is, and exchange the lie for the life-giving truth of God's better path. In his book titled *Orthodoxy*, G. K. Chesterton made the point long ago that until we make such a decision, we will continue to live the life of a madman believing all is well when in actuality we are insane. Is it not insane to go on living as if we know better than the God of the universe? Chesterton wrote: "People have fallen into a foolish habit of speaking of orthodoxy as something heavy, humdrum, and safe. There was never anything so perilous or so exciting as orthodoxy. It was sanity: and to be sane is more dramatic than to be mad." Amidst the madness of Hurricane Katrina and other such disasters, God is calling us back to sanity.

We need to hear the admonition of Ravi Zacharias in his book *Can Man Live Without God* as he comments on the pitiful existence of one of the most important philosophers in recent history and the correlation to our approach to life here in the Western world. Referring to the committed atheist, Friedrich Nietzsche, who made every attempt to live out his nihilistic philosophy in practical terms, and who in the end went absolutely mad, Zacharias wrote:

> He may turn out to be the most important philosopher of the
> last two centuries because he tried in practical terms to answer
> the greatest question of our time in his own being. . . . In his
> dreadful condition of madness, he possibly embodied and
> foreshadowed the lunacy unto death that seems to possess
> Western civilization today as it denies the very idea of God
> and any access into the lives of this generation.

Nietzsche's life and his lunacy, upon historical review, certainly
bear a shocking resemblance to our current preoccupation with the
abandonment of absolute truth and our national craving to live life
for the moment. Our quest for more of everything, our dependence upon unending entertainment, and our societal addiction to
sex, all seem to be leading us toward a madness of soul that is
frighteningly similar to that of Nietzsche and those who proclaimed along with him, "God is dead."

In barring the living God from our national conscience we are in
danger of imprisoning our own souls as a people. Yet, we wish to
call ourselves a "Christian" nation. We seem intent on having the
protection of the Divine while despising His proclamations. We
assert that God the Armor Bearer is on our side, yet we bar His
presence from our schools, our courts, our bedrooms, and our
hearts. Again Ravi wrote in that same book:

> God has been barred from the institutions that determine soci-
> ety's thinking and behavior. I, for one, see Nietzsche's life and
> death as a blueprint for where we are headed inexorably as a
> nation, having committed ourselves to an antitheistic form of
> government and education.

Lest we should think the link is a bit too far-reaching, we need
only to turn to CNN to find just how true the link really is. The
further we remove God from the center of our society, the more
likely we are to find ever-increasing insanity among us. As
Westerners, we often point to our relative moral goodness as we
aim our accusing finger across the oceans, where true madness

took place during the Holocaust. We must recognize, however, that the devaluation of life that saw its logical unfolding in those dark days has taken root in our society, though perhaps in different form. The philosophical roots are the same.

Sobering words are found in the writings of Viktor Frankl, who survived the madness of the death camps. In *The Doctor and the Soul* he wrote, "I am absolutely convinced that the gas chambers of Auschwitz, Treblinka, and Maidanek were ultimately prepared not in some ministry or other in Berlin, but rather at the desks and in lecture halls of nihilistic scientists and philosophers." These are important words for a culture wrestling with the debates over abortion, euthanasia, and stem-cell research. God is speaking amidst our disasters. Are we listening? Are we willing to change? Can we rebuild a better way?

The Providence of God

Ultimately, Katrina's message and the message of this book are about the providence of God in our lives. It is a message of God's care, direction, purposes, and hand. Whether we believe God sent Katrina, allowed Katrina, or is merely working through Katrina, the reality is the same. He is at work. He is always at work in the events of our lives. Romans 8:28 (NIV) assures us that God is working in and through all things to bring about His purposes in our lives. Even those things that are meant for evil God turns around and uses for good. This is one of the grand themes of scripture.

Hard times, we are told, separate the men from the boys, the wheat from the chaff, and the good from the bad. The Bible tells us that life's difficulties are what God uses to "refine" us, just as precious metals are refined by the testing of fire (Zech. 13:9). Hebrews chapter 11 tells us of the "faithful" servants of God who trusted, fought, and endured for the purposes of God, having never received the promise on this side of heaven. The life, and blindness, of one of history's greatest writers, John Milton, demonstrates to us that "they also serve who only stand and wait." And the life of Joseph reminds us that even the evil intent of those around us cannot thwart the purposes of God for a life devoted to Him (Gen. 50:20).

As you may recall, Joseph's brothers, envious and embittered over their father's preference for the boy, devised a plan to put him to death. In God's providence, the plan was altered, and they sold him into slavery. By "chance," those who originally purchased him sold him into the hands and household of the master of Egypt. Through God's orchestration, Joseph found favor in the household, and was elevated to a place of high esteem. Once there, the master's wife attempted to seduce him. Upon his refusal to give in, she lied and had him defamed and thrown into prison. But God was not done.

While in prison, Joseph remained convinced of God's love and committed to His purposes. He eventually found favor as He lived a godly life amidst criminals. After being found to have the gift of dream interpretation, and after a rather lengthy delay in his quest for freedom, he made it out. Through it all, God brought him back to a place of prominence in Pharaoh's house, and one telling verse screams of divine ability to turn the worst of life's messes into God's grace-filled plan. Genesis 41:57 reads, "All the earth came to Egypt to Joseph to buy grain, because the famine was severe over all the earth." In the end, the whole of civilization came looking for hope and help from the little bothersome brother, slave, prisoner, and prude!

Has Hurricane Katrina changed everything for you? Is your soul in distress? Where has your life gone "right" and where has your life gone "wrong?" Whether you have seen victory after victory or defeat upon defeat, hold steady in the arms of God and trust that He is up to something. If you place yourself in His hands, and like Job, wrestle through the tough questions long enough to see that no one knows better than God, you will come to see the hand of providence.

Remember, throughout biblical history, it seems that those who walked with God in the most intimate of ways endured much hardship. Do you want to experience the providential hand of God in your life? His favor is assured, and His blessings are many, and we ought to praise Him for each one. He longs to give good gifts to His sons and daughters. Let us also be mindful, however, that sometimes the "best" of His plans are drawn up on the blueprint of suffering. Jeremiah was the "weeping prophet;" Hosea was called to marry a prostitute; Isaiah was undone, and lived among an unclean, rebellious people; Paul was imprisoned, beaten, ship-wrecked, and left for dead numerous times; Daniel was thrown into a den of lions; John the baptizer wore a really irritating shirt and ate some obnoxiously noisy bugs; and Jesus, who endured the most severe soul storm ever encountered, bearing the weight of the world's sin upon His soul, and who cried out to the Father, "Why have you forsaken me?" (Matt. 47:26) was the Suffering Servant.

He is Emmanuel, "God with us" (Matt. 1:23 KJV). He withstood the storm of the cross, was raised from the dead, and lives forever-more. He remains forever as the One who continually makes inter-cession on our behalf before the Father (Heb. 7:24-25).

Jesus, the Man, is more than our example, He is God in the flesh, and He shows us the way through the disasters of our lives. He is our bridge to safety. There exists no other way to freedom and life. Jesus, and Jesus alone, is our salvation from the greatest storm, which awaits us at the grave. Through Him, as our Shepherd, we find our way through the valley of death (Ps. 23:1, 4).

If we are to deal realistically with the disasters of this life, and if we are to find sanity amidst our success, we must deal with this Man and His claims. Upon this Man, and upon this event, the Christ event, all of history finds its purpose. In Him and in Him alone, the suffering of this world finds its redemption.

The words of C. S. Lewis are an intelligent and powerful clarion call to find our shelter from the storms of life in this Man who walked the earth just two thousand years ago. In *Mere Christianity*, Lewis reminds us that Jesus cannot simply be dismissed as a great moral teacher or a good man. As Lewis suggests, anyone who claims the sort of things Jesus claimed, particularly that He was the son of God, would be considered mentally ill, a pathological liar, or a demon possessed. We are forced to make a choice about this man. Lewis writes,

> Either this man was, and is, the Son of God: or else a madman or something worse. You can shut Him up for a fool, you can spit at Him and kill Him as a demon; or you can fall at His feet and call Him Lord and God.

Until and unless we embrace this truth, the soul storm will not abate. God has made provision and provided rescue. To refuse this way to safety is to invite our own ruin. In running to this shelter we will find "the pearl of great price" (Matt. 13:45-46 KJV), "the treasure hidden in a field" (Matt. 13:44), the divine romance.

God is indeed found amidst disaster. More appropriately, amidst the disasters of our lives, God finds us. He hunts for us, He moves on our behalf, and He directs the storms that they might call us unto Him. Lost things matter to God. Lost people, lost dreams, and lost purposes are restored by His touch. May we learn to be found in Him no matter the storm, no matter the price, and for the joy set before us in knowing, loving, and enjoying Him forever. Amen.

Also available as a companion to *Soul Storm: Finding God Amidst Disaster*

Music for the Soul presents *After the Storm*, a CD of hope and encouragement for the people of the Gulf Coast. The CD includes songs written and performed by residents of New Orleans, vocal performances by Larnelle Harris, Lisa Bevill, and Scott Krippayne, and interviews with evacuees.

"This CD is the gospel of Jesus Christ. It hits home."

— Larry Roques, pastor, New Orleans

Music for the Soul is a not-for-profit Christian organization creating issue-specific CDs that combine song and spoken word to bring hope to those dealing with life's most difficult challenges.

Steve Siler, director of Music for the Soul, is an accomplished songwriter and musical producer. Over 500 of his songs have been recorded in the Christian, pop, and country music markets by artists such as Kenny Loggins, Smokey Robinson, Patti LaBelle, the Oak Ridge Boys, and many others. He has been nominated for four Dove Awards, winning the award in 2000 for Inspirational Song of the Year.